MW00855755

COFFEE
ROASTING

COFFEE
ROASTING

— BEST PRACTICES —

Scott Rao

I'd like to thank the wonderful Jaroslavs of Prague's Doubleshot Coffee for generously allowing David, Neli, and me to use their roastery and café for our photo shoots.

The author has taken care in preparing this book but assumes no responsibility for errors or inaccuracies.
Copyright 2020 Scott Rao
All rights reserved. No part of this book may be used or reproduced in any manner whatsoever without written permission, except in the case of brief quotations embodied in critical articles or reviews.

Text by Scott Rao
Editing by Jean Zimmer
Photographs on pages 17, 21, 24, 36, 44, 51, 57, 67, 68, 74, 76, 80, and 84 copyright 2019 by
    David Zidlicky
Charts and graphs by Janine Aniko Manlangit
Illustrations by Kathryn Avansino
Book and cover design by Rebecca S. Neimark, Twenty-Six Letters

Printed in China
ISBN 978-1-7923-2775-9

Please visit www.scottrao.com for information about Scott's books and consulting services.

Table of Contents

Preface   ix
Introduction   xi

1   How To Approach a New Coffee   1
How to approach roasting an unfamiliar bean
How a coffee's physical attributes affect its roasting
Bean size
Moisture content and water activity
Density
Bean shape
The upshot

2   Basic Coffee Chemistry and Roasting   5
Physical changes during roasting
The "drying phase"
Browning reactions
Development time
Carbonization
Roast development

3   Quality Data Collection   9
Gas manometer
Temperature probes
Proper probe size and location

4   Tuning Your Roaster   13
Drum rpm
Setting airflow
Gas pressure
Burner tuning

5   Preparation and Consistency   17
Consistent results
Green-coffee temperature

Warming up a roaster
Managing roastery temperature in winter
Between-batch protocol (BBP)
Mastering repeatability
Planning a roast day

6 Setting Reasonable Parameters 24
Batch size
Charge temperature
Roast time

7 Reading Roast Curves 27
The unmanaged roast
Baked roasts
The flick
The smoothly declining ROR
Development time ratio (DTR): what it means, and what it doesn't

8 How Probe Speed and Location Influence Curves 34
Art vs. science
Data interpretation
Optimal probe size
Probe speed and ROR curve shape
Trends vs. events

9 Airflow Management 42
Dampers vs. variable-speed fans
No airflow adjustments required
One or more adjustments on drum roasters
Machines requiring airflow management

10 Basic Gas Management 44
Charge with high gas, and lower the gas stepwise as the batch progresses
The soak
Basic ROR management approaching first crack
Fixing "soft" ROR crashes
Fixing "hard" ROR crashes
Adjusting the gas after first crack
When to adjust the gas during first crack
Inlet temperature

11 The Phases of Moisture Release and the Gas Dip 53
The phases of moisture release
How to manage gas settings based on the phases of moisture release
The gas dip method
Why the gas dip works

12 Marking First Crack Using the ETROR Curve   62

13 Odds and Ends   64
Strategies for indirectly heated roasters
Using electric roasters
Why I don't care to manage the time spent in the so-called Maillard phase
Roasting for filter vs. espresso
Roasting for "black coffee" vs. "white coffee"

14 Post-Roast Quality Control   69
Color measurement
Measuring weight loss
Other indicators of roast development

15 Sample Roasting and Cupping   72
Sample roasting
What you can (and can't) learn from a sample roast's data
How to cup
Cupping "espresso roasts"
Cupping right out of the roaster

16 Bean Storage   78
Green-coffee packaging
Green storage and longevity
Green storage and roast repeatability
Roasted-coffee storage
Storing ground coffee

17 Common Roasting Mistakes and Hindrances   81
Too much data smoothing
Thick probes
Roasting too many different batch sizes
Inconsistent or ineffective between-batch protocol
Self-satisfaction, inadequate blind cupping, and cupping of others' coffees

18 Roasting Software and Automation   84
Types of roasting software
Simple data-logging freeware (for non-techies)
Sophisticated freeware for data logging and other tasks
Commercial roastery management solutions
Integrated software
How to choose software for your needs
Roast control and automation
Manual roasting
Recipe software systems (semiautomated control)
Automated profiling systems (fully automatic control)

19 Software Setup and Troubleshooting 88
Things to consider before connecting your roaster
What you'll need to connect
Choosing a computer for your roastery
How to connect your computer
How to confirm everything is working
Troubleshooting connections and data
Expert hints and simple mistakes to avoid

Glossary 91

Preface

When I wrote *The Coffee Roaster's Companion* (*CRC*) in 2014, it was difficult to know how to present my ideas on roasting. At the time, there were no books about professional roasting. The coffee industry lacked much of the shared vocabulary and understanding needed to have productive discussions about roasting, and most roasters seemed hesitant to share their ideas, perhaps due to fear of giving away secrets or fear of being wrong.

I wasn't sure how much knowledge or experience most readers would have, so I wrote *The Coffee Roaster's Companion* in a form I hoped would benefit roasters of all levels. In the past four years, roasters worldwide have adopted concepts from *CRC* such as *development time ratio* and *constantly declining rate of rise (ROR)*, and as a group we are having more coherent and practical conversations about roasting than ever before.

When I wrote *CRC* I had used about 100 roasting machines, which gave me a unique, rounded perspective on the roasting process. As of this writing, I have used well over 300 machines and analyzed roasting data from hundreds more. That broad experience helped me form advanced ideas about roasting that would not have been possible had I used merely a handful of machines. This book is the product of my experience, and I hope your roasting skills benefit as I share with you what I learned.

Introduction

I wrote this book for experienced coffee roasters. I assume the reader knows the basic parts of a roasting machine and common roasting terminology and is at least vaguely familiar with *bean-temperature* and *ROR curves.* The early chapters discuss the needed equipment, software, and accessories. The middle chapters describe how to tune a roasting machine, how to ensure consistent results, and how to analyze a roast curve. The later chapters of the book are packed with advanced ideas about gas management, manipulation of roast curves, and post-roast quality control.

The goal of this book is to offer you a system for efficiently developing coffee with as few roast defects as possible. If applied as a whole, and with a little practice, this system will work—it has worked for hundreds of my clients, many of whom are among the world's most respected roasters. I hope readers will embrace this system with an open mind and be willing to put in the time and effort to make it work for them.

Scott Rao
California, 2019

1

How To Approach a New Coffee

I'm not an expert at buying *green coffee*. I can tell the difference between an 86- and an 87-point coffee, but being a skilled green buyer requires much more than a refined palate, and I know many pros whose green-buying skills far exceed mine. The art of buying green coffee deserves—and has—its own book: *Dear Coffee Buyer* by Ryan Brown. I support every word of that book and strongly recommend that you read it if you ever plan to buy green coffee or work in the coffee industry. There is little I can add to the green-buying wisdom of *Dear Coffee Buyer*, so I won't spill any ink here on issues related to buying green coffee.

Coffee beans on branch

Instead, let's assume you have some roasting experience, you've read *Dear Coffee Buyer* six times cover to cover, and you're tasked with roasting an unfamiliar bean. How should you approach it?

How to approach roasting an unfamiliar bean

A roaster has three tools at her disposal when deciding how to roast a new coffee:

- Personal experience: After roasting thousands of batches, a roaster gains a mental database of beans and how they behaved during roasting. When faced with a new coffee, a roaster can draw from previous experience to anticipate the settings and timing needed to roast the new bean well. For example, an experienced roaster may

know to decrease gas settings when roasting a naturally processed coffee or an exceptionally small bean.
- Sample roasting: Before the first *production roast* of a coffee, a roaster may choose to sample roast the bean to get a sense of how it will roast. A sample roast can offer useful, but limited, insight into how to manage a bean. Please see Chapter 15 for an extensive discussion of sample roasting.
- Measuring the bean's physical attributes: Several physical attributes affect how a green coffee will roast; the most important are the beans' size, shape, density, and *moisture content*. When planning the settings of a roast, I consider those traits as well as the batch size and how the beans were processed (natural, washed, etc.).

Ideally, a roaster should track as many of these physical attributes as possible for each lot of coffee she roasts. Once she has amassed a large enough database of measured beans, she can reference it to find the closest analog for each new arrival. The settings she used for a previous successful roast offer a useful starting point for the new coffee.

Given that such a database would be complex and take a long time to establish, I'll suggest this shortcut: focus heavily on bean size and moisture content. Those two attributes vary widely, so they often have the greatest impact on optimal roast settings. When planning to roast an unfamiliar coffee, find a past analog that had similar bean size and moisture content and adopt the analog's most successful settings, adjusted according to your experience.

How a coffee's physical attributes affect its roasting

When roasters tell me how they approach a new bean, they refer most often to its processing (e.g., natural or washed) and density. While those are two important considerations, I'd like to offer this section to widen the range of factors roasters should consider when assessing how to roast a new coffee.

Bean size

All else being equal, larger beans require more energy to roast. If a roaster references gas settings on a scale of 0% to 100%, she may choose to use, for instance, a peak gas setting of 80% for a Kenya AA but only 65% for a Kenya peaberry from the same farm, in order to roast both coffees to the same degree in a similar time frame.

Moisture content and water activity

Moisture content is the proportion of a bean's weight made up of water. Moister beans generally require more energy to roast, and they release more water vapor during a batch. That vapor cools the bean surfaces and impedes heat transfer into the beans, likely by deflecting some of the approaching hot air. Higher moisture content also increases a bean's *thermal conductivity*, which by itself would increase the rate of heat transfer into the bean, but that effect is outweighed by the cooling and deflecting effects of additional moisture.

Typical green-coffee moisture content is in the range of 8%–12%; moisture content below that range often results in hollow, straw-like coffee flavor (though a few origins tend to be delicious at low moisture contents). Moisture content above 12% may yield flavorful coffee, but with time the green coffee is more likely to harbor microbial overgrowth, which may damage flavor or (speculatively) the health of the consumer.

Water activity (a_w) and moisture content are different, but they are correlated. Wikipedia defines a_w as *the partial vapor pressure of water in a substance divided by the standard state partial vapor pressure of water.* In layman's terms, a_w refers to the amount of "free" (unbound) water in a food relative to its bound water. Microbes need water for growth; a greater variety of microbes can thrive in food products with higher a_w.

The range of a_w in specialty coffee is perhaps 0.45–0.65; high-quality beans measure about 0.53–0.59. Given this small range and water activity's high correlation with moisture content, it is difficult to isolate the influence of water activity (a_w) on the energy required to roast a bean.

Although I can't offer any words of wisdom about how to use a_w levels to adjust energy during a roast, I recommend trying to buy green coffee with a_w in the range of 0.53–0.59. You may find lovely coffees with a_w outside of that range, but coffees in that range tend to taste great and age more gracefully.

Density

Denser beans require more energy to roast. For example, a dense Guatemalan bean grown at an altitude of 1500 meters requires noticeably more gas to roast than will a similarly sized, less-dense bean grown in Brazil at 500 meters. This is an important consideration for roasters who use beans of a wide range of quality. However, a roaster who deals only in high-altitude-grown, high-quality specialty coffee can be lax in tracking bean density, as it will rarely vary enough to impact the choice of gas settings.

To measure density without using expensive equipment, one may use the common methods of *bulk density* and *displacement*. To take a bulk-density measurement, fill a container of known volume with coffee beans, weigh the beans, and divide the weight by the container's volume. Bulk-density measurements are convenient but imprecise; they can be misleading, as bean size and shape influence how tightly beans pack into a given space. To measure density by displacement, fill a container of known volume with a weighed dose of coffee beans and then add a filler, such as water, to fill the container completely and determine how much volume the beans displaced.

Bean shape

Let's consider two extremes to illustrate the effect of bean shape on roasting: a perfectly spherical bean and a bean shaped like a rectangular brick, both of the same volume. Of all potential bean shapes, a spherical bean would have the lowest possible surface-area-to-volume ratio and the longest minimum path from the bean surface to the bean center. The brick's center would be easier to develop, in that the shortest distance from the surface to the center would be much shorter than that of the sphere. However, the brick would be more prone to *tipping, scorching,* and uneven development. The high surface-area-to-volume ratio of the brick's corners make them likely to tip, and the areas near them are likely to scorch. Coffee beans may never be shaped exactly like bricks or spheres, but these extreme examples illustrate that rounder beans are easier to roast evenly, without undesirable roast taints.

The upshot

There is no simple formula to predict how to approach a roast of an unfamiliar bean. But rather than merely guess at settings, an experienced roaster can take a systematic approach. He can combine data from a sample roast of the coffee, physical measurements of the green coffee, and insights gained from roasting similar coffees to approach the first batch of new coffee with confidence and potentially promising settings.

2

Basic Coffee Chemistry and Roasting

Roasters love to discuss *Maillard reactions*, *caramelization*, "the drying phase," and other bits of roasting chemistry. But rarely in such conversations will you hear practical, accurate advice on how to apply our knowledge of roasting chemistry to improve flavor. We collectively know perhaps 1% of what there is to know about roasting chemistry, and what we do know is usually difficult or impossible to apply in practice. In this chapter, I discuss basic facts of roasting chemistry, but I offer it more for general interest than as practical advice. Books and scientific papers that address the minutiae of roasting chemistry are easy to find; if that subject interests you, then by all means, dive in. Just don't expect that education to make you a much better coffee roaster.

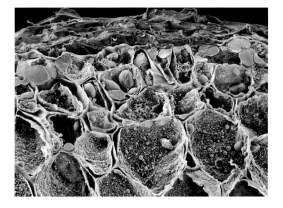

A coffee bean's structure is a matrix of cellulose strands that crisscross to form approximately 1,000,000 cells or void spaces. Various solids and oils coat the cellulose, and water typically makes up 8%–12% of a bean's weight. If you had known how ugly coffee is under a microscope, would you still love it so much?

Physical changes during roasting

The most obvious physical effects of roasting include the browning, expansion, and dehydration of coffee beans. During roasting, beans lose moisture, build pressure at their interiors, almost double in volume, and lose weight. The simultaneous expansion and weight loss cause beans' density to decrease by half during roasting.

Roasting creates water and also drives off the vast majority of the water in coffee beans. Moisture content of roasted coffee will typically range between 1%–2%, with all, or almost all, of that moisture bound to the cellulose structure. Net weight loss during roasting depends on a roast batch's initial moisture content and the degree of roast. Weight loss measurements may range from 13%–15% for a light *third-wave roast* to greater than 20% for an early–*second crack* roast, such as that typical of Starbucks, to almost 25% for unspeakably dark roasts.

Many of the chemicals present in green coffee also exist in roasted beans, and many new compounds are formed during roasting. Some highlights of the chemical changes of roasting include

- Breakdown of chlorogenic acids
- Destruction of almost all of the free sucrose present in green coffee
- Creation of long-chain sugar molecules, or polysaccharides
- Breakdown of polysaccharides into simpler sugars
- Reactions between sugars and amino acids to produce coffee's "roasty" flavors
- Browning of sugars by caramelization
- In dark roasts, *carbonization* of organic material

Contrary to popular belief, while a tiny amount of caffeine is lost during roasting, the proportion, by weight, of caffeine in coffee beans increases as beans lose weight during roasting. Thus, if you brew a light roast and a dark roast to the same strength using the same brewing ratio, the dark roast's brew will contain more caffeine.

Gases created during roasting create pressure within the beans. Although researchers disagree profoundly on how much pressure builds up in beans leading up to *first crack*, the median estimate is approximately 10 atmospheres. As roasting weakens beans' cellulose structures and increases pressure at their cores, a tipping point is reached wherein the pressure is too great for the weakening structures. This tipping point triggers first crack, an audible fracturing of bean structures and release of gases—primarily water vapor—from the beans.

First crack begins slowly, accelerates, slows again, and lasts anywhere from 1 to 3 minutes. Shortly after first crack ends, second crack begins. Second crack consists of yet another release of gases, this time primarily carbon dioxide, triggered by further weakening and fracturing of the cellulose structure. Around the time

second crack begins, oil seeps from some bean surfaces, another indicator of the increasing pressure within beans overcoming their weakening structures.

The "drying phase"

Many roasters refer to the first few minutes of a batch as the "drying phase," a term that is a little misleading. Beans release little to no moisture during the first 60–90 seconds of a (typical) roast because none of the bean mass has reached vaporization (boiling) temperature. During the next few minutes, beans release moisture at a high and steady rate, as successively deeper layers of bean mass reach vaporization temperature and release steam.

Browning reactions

As a roast leaves the "drying phase" it enters two successive phases of nonenzymatic browning reactions: the Maillard phase followed by caramelization. Once the moisture content of the beans is low enough, Maillard reactions begin.

Maillard reactions occur between various reducing sugars and amino acids during roasting. Much is made of the Maillard phase of roasting, as Maillard reactions produce a great deal of coffee's flavor, aromatics, and complexity. The most well-known such flavors include those reminiscent of toasted bread and grilled meat.

While Maillard reactions are critical to coffee flavor, many roasters overreach in their assumptions about the relationship between flavor and time spent in the Maillard phase of roasting. Please see Chapter 13 for more on that topic.

As the Maillard phase winds down, caramelization takes over. Caramelization browns beans further, creates new aromatics, breaks down beans' little remaining free sugar, and enhances coffee's bittersweet quality.

Development time

As caramelization continues and first crack begins, a roast enters a phase known as *development (time)*.

As with the other roast-phase labels, "development time" can be misleading. Strictly speaking, development time refers to the amount of time between the beginning of first crack and the end of a roast. I'd like to dissuade readers from thinking that more development time means more *roast development*. The relationship between development time and roast development is not so simple.

Carbonization

Should one choose to roast past the middle of second crack, carbonization will blacken the beans. Though I will not judge others for enjoying coffee roasted so darkly, I will say I'm grateful that the popularity of dark, carbonized coffee has declined over the past couple of decades, the efforts of Peet's, Starbucks, and their copycats notwithstanding. Such roasts not only destroy varietal character and nuance, but they also push coffee oils to the bean surfaces, where the oils quickly turn rancid. Rancidity is both unpalatable and unhealthy for the consumer and so it should be avoided.

Roast development

We call the process of breaking down beans' cellulose "roast development." As a roast develops, the cellulose, initially rubbery, becomes more brittle and porous. Brittleness is necessary for beans to shatter effectively during grinding, and porosity is required for liquid to pass into and out of ground-particle cells during brewing. When beans are not as brittle or porous as desired, we say a roast is *underdeveloped*. Underdeveloped coffee may yield vegetal aromas and low extractions during brewing. Note that roast development is not simply a matter of roasting beans darker on the outside. Although that is the easiest way to increase development, a skilled roaster can produce a very light roast on the outside with no hints of underdevelopment on the inside. We will now focus on how you can enhance roast development while minimizing roast defects in your coffee.

3

Quality Data Collection

I wrote this book for those who currently have a roasting machine or at least some roasting experience. If you are a novice interested in buying a roasting machine, please read my upcoming e-book *How to Choose a Roasting Machine*. I discuss various features and upgrades to consider when purchasing a machine.

I've limited this chapter to a discussion of the two most important features that should be—but aren't always—standard on a machine: a precision gas *manometer* and a properly sized, properly placed *bean-temperature probe*. These features are critical because they track the main input and output of a roast: the manometer measures the gas pressure, or the input, and the bean probe tracks bean temperature, the most important output. If your machine lacks one of these features, I strongly recommend upgrading to it on your machine.

You may wonder why roasting-machine manufacturers would build machines without prioritizing these two features. The reason is historical: widespread use of roast-data-logging software began only 10 or 12 years ago. Before data logging became popular, few roasters saw a need for precision data collection, so machines were built with one slow, thick bean probe or with no bean probe at all!

In the early days of data logging, manufacturers ignored customer requests for better probes and manometers. Meanwhile, intrepid home roasters modified their own machines, posted their data online, and spread awareness of the value of precision roast data. Over the past 10 years, the manufacturers have, each in their own way, modernized their machines' data collection system.

There is much work to be done, as some popular machines still lack appropriate probes and manometers. Even if you have a new machine with high-tech features, please read this chapter and check that your machine is optimized for quality data collection.

Gas manometer

A roaster needs to know exactly how much gas she is applying at all times during a roast*, but many machines lack a manometer that reads active gas usage. Specifically, I'm referring to a manometer placed between the gas valve and burner. Of the machines that come with such manometers, many have resolution too low

---

* This is not strictly true, as a roaster could rely on an *inlet-temperature (IT)* probe in lieu of gas-pressure reading, but that discussion is beyond the scope of this book.

Left: Although an analog manometer has aesthetic appeal, its readings are more difficult to discern with precision. For example, this roaster's burner maxes out at 20 mbar, which is a fraction of the manometer's range. To repeat roasts with precision, it's important to be able to discern between settings as close as 10.1 and 10.2 during a batch, but I doubt any human could achieve such precision with this device. **Right:** A good digital manometer offers measurements with programmable smoothing to prevent noisy readings and to provide exactly the desired amount of precision.

to be very useful. For example, a roaster's normal range of gas pressure may be 0–8 *inches of water column*, but its manometer may read from 0–25 inches of wc. In other words, all of the potential readings are clustered within a small section of the manometer's dial, making precise readings and repeatability impossible. It's beyond the scope of this book to dive into the details of various manometers, but it is worth the reader's time to learn about them and ensure he chooses an appropriate one. At the very least, source a quality digital manometer to improve the precision of your measurements.

Your machine may lack a precision manometer but track "gas %" on your machine's control panel. The percent readings on such systems do not usually indicate gas pressure; they indicate valve settings. In other words, "30%" may indicate the gas valve is 30% open. The problem with such a system is that if the machine's incoming gas pressure changes, the burner's power output will change as well, but the panel will still read "30%." If your incoming gas pressure never fluctuates, this system can work well.

Incoming gas pressure may change frequently throughout the day (if the roasting machine shares a gas line with other equipment), seasonally, or almost never. If your incoming gas pressure fluctuates regularly, your roasting results will be inconsistent, and you may have no idea why. If you have this sort of fluctuating control system, consider adding an incoming manometer and a regulator to ensure the machine's incoming pressure never changes.

Temperature probes

RTDs and *thermocouple* types such as J and K are all well suited to roasting. An effective probe is responsive and well located. A probe's response speed is related to its diameter: thinner probes are generally faster than thicker probes, as thinner probes have less thermal mass and therefore change temperature more quickly. Roasting manufacturers often prefer to install thicker probes, probably because they are less likely to break, but sometimes because of ignorance—they may not understand the value of faster, more accurate bean-temperature data. When I've advocated for faster probes, many manufacturers have argued it doesn't matter; others have become genuinely curious because no one had ever asked them for that.

Similarly, manufacturers often choose to install a probe near the drum's center axle (i.e., far from the inner edge of the drum). Such a probe may be immersed in the bean pile during a full batch, but it may not provide accurate bean-temperature data for smaller batches because its tip won't be immersed in the bean pile.

Proper probe size and location

I recommend using probes of approximately 2.5–4-mm diameter. In my experience, thicker probes are often too slow, and thinner probes are often too noisy. Approximately 3-mm diameter is the sweet spot for a balance of speed and noise.

It's important to position the probe so its tip will be in the heart of the bean pile, even when you are roasting very small batches. If the tip is too central in the machine (i.e., near the axle), the beans may rotate away from it periodically during a batch, causing volatile bean-temperature data. Batch size and drum rpm (revolutions per minute) affect the location of the bean pile, so it's best to play it safe with probe location by ensuring the tip will be immersed in the bean pile of even the smallest batch.

For small machines, I recommend installing the probe tip 2–3 cm from the inner edge of the drum and 2–3 cm from the faceplate. For larger machines (12-kg and above) I recommend installing the tip 3–4 cm from both the faceplate and inner-drum edge.

Before drilling any holes,

When the probe is too close to the machine's center axle, it may not provide accurate temperature readings in smaller batches.

it is imperative to ensure the new probe location won't interfere with the machine's *mixing vanes*. Once you are confident the new location is safe, drill the hole with the machine off, turn on the machine, and gently slide a breakable wooden or plastic stir stick through the hole to determine the safe bean-probe depth.

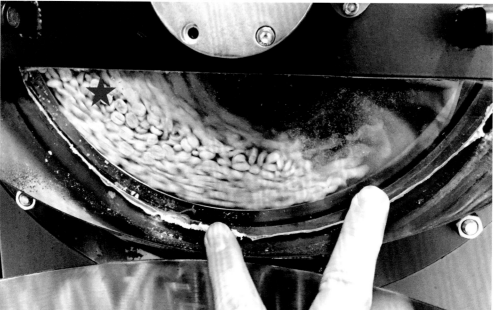

Top: Perfect probe placement in a drum that turns counterclockwise. **Bottom:** My friend Mark replaced his roaster's metal door with a clear-plastic door in order to see the location of the bean pile at different batch sizes and drum rpms. The star indicates an ideal location for a bean probe.

4

Tuning Your Roaster

When clients hire me to consult on their roasting, they usually expect we'll jump into improving roast curves the moment we begin. While I wish all jobs could work out that way, and some do, I usually find that clients' machines are not tuned properly for optimal roasting. Tuning the machine and having the tools to collect quality roast data are prerequisites for consistently great roasting. Please address these concerns prior to attempting to finesse roast curves.

The most common problems I see include slow, poorly located temperature probes, improper drum rpm, and inadequate gas pressure. These problems are so common that substandard installations are the norm, not the exception. Once we address these problems, we are ready to rapidly improve roasting results. While it's necessary to confirm probe size and location only once, the best roasters I know inspect probe tightness and cleanliness, drum rpm, and gas pressure on a regular basis.

Drum rpm

Proper drum rpm (revolutions per minute) is essential for even mixing of beans during roasting, minimizing scorching and tipping (the side effects of too much *conductive heat transfer*), and ensuring adequate *convective heat transfer*. Please do not assume the factory set your new roaster's drum rpm properly. A few manufacturers have poor track records, often delivering the same model of machine at a wide variety of rpms.

For *classic-drum roasters*, drum diameter is the primary determinant of optimal rpm. Given that different brands of machines have different drum proportions (i.e., some 15-kg drums are wide and shallow, and others are narrow and deep), the recommended ranges in the chart below are estimates, not hard rules.

If the drum's rpms are too low or too high, beans will rest against the drum wall for too long during each revolution, which increases the risk

MACHINE CAPACITY	DRUM RPM
1–2 kg	70–80 rpm
5–7 kg	60–70 rpm
12 kg	52–56 rpm
15 kg	50–54 rpm
30 kg	46–50 rpm

of tipping and scorching. Drum rpms in the proper range offer the best chance of clean, soft-tasting coffee with minimal defects.

Setting airflow

During roasting, *airflow* serves to exhaust heat, smoke, and chaff and to provide convective heat transfer. Using too little airflow makes coffee smoky; other than that, airflow does not directly affect flavor. When you change airflow settings batch to batch, it indirectly affects the flavor of the coffee by altering the balance of incoming versus outgoing heat and changing the shapes of the *bean curve* and *ROR curves*.

While I cannot tell you precisely how much airflow to use in your roasting, the following indicators will ensure your airflow is in a reasonably good range. The recommendations apply to classic-drum roasters only. If you have an *indirectly heated roaster*, please see Chapter 13 for notes on airflow management in such machines. If you have a Loring roaster, you should also skip this chapter, as the machine's airflow management and burner tuning are preset by the factory.

Use the "cigarette-lighter test" to adjust airflow in a classic-drum roaster. To do the test, hold a cigarette lighter 1 centimeter from the *trier* hole approximately halfway through a roast. Light the flame, remove the trier, and note the angle at which the flame leans toward the hole. If the air from the hole pushes the flame away, airflow is set much too low. If the flame leans toward the hole at an angle of 60–90 degrees, airflow is reasonable. If suction from the hole snuffs the flame, the airflow is likely set too high. The test's "reasonable" range will ensure your airflow level is appropriate, if not optimal.

Use enough airflow to ensure efficient removal of smoke and chaff from the

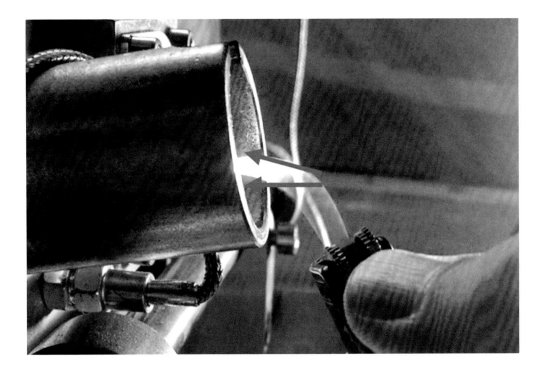

Either this batch's airflow was set too low or the roast was extremely dark.

drum and to avoid trapping too much heat late in the roast. If a lot of smoke wafts out of the drum upon discharging a batch or a noticeable amount of chaff mixes with the beans in the cooling bin, the airflow may be set too low.

It's difficult to tell if the airflow is set excessively high on a roasting machine. The airflow may fail the cigarette lighter test, but that is a crude indicator. When the airflow is much too high, the perceptive roaster will notice clues such as *environmental-temperature (ET)* curves peaking early and falling before first crack, *ROR crashes* becoming difficult to fix, and roast times extending slightly longer than usual.

If your roaster doesn't already have one, I recommend installing a manometer to measure air pressure in the duct between the drum and the exhaust fan. Air pressure is a useful proxy for airflow, and having a manometer will help you maintain consistent airflow levels from day to day as the weather changes. I recommend finding a manometer capable of sending a digital signal to your roasting software for automatic logging of air-pressure readings.

Gas pressure

Your roaster likely has a metal badge somewhere on its side, listing the electrical and gas requirements. Most machine manufacturers' websites also list their roasters' electrical and gas requirements. A surprising number of clients have had too little gas pressure before I began working with them, so please take a moment to learn your machine's gas requirements. Inadequate gas pressure limits batch capacity and slows roasts. Prior to machine installation, check that your gas pressure and gas-line diameter are appropriate for your machine. The optimal gas pressure is the top of the manufacturers' recommended range. In other words, if the manufacturer recommends 3–5 kpa, try to bring 5 kpa to your machine.

If you're unsure of your current gas pressure, rest assured that if you can roast a 75%-capacity batch in fewer than 12 minutes with a reasonable airflow setting and *charge* temperature, your gas pressure is probably adequate.

Burner tuning

Many newer roasters have "fuel-injected" burners that control the air–fuel ratio to ensure optimal combustion. Upon delivery of a machine, a technician should tune the burner to the optimal ratio. Compared with the atmospheric burners common on older roasters, these modern burners offer greater fuel efficiency and lower emissions.

When using a roaster with an atmospheric burner, be mindful that changing the airflow through the drum affects both roasting and combustion quality. It is usually easy to find a range of airflow settings that yields a clean, blue flame and quality roasting. If you cannot produce a clean, predominantly blue flame with normal roast-airflow settings, contact the machine's manufacturer. If the flame is steady and blue, the air–fuel ratio is probably reasonable.

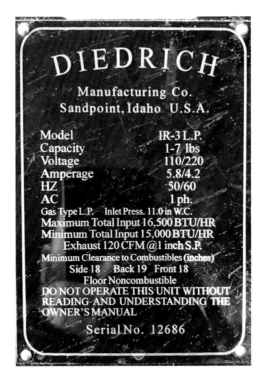

Most roasting machines have a metal badge stamped on their side that indicates gas and electrical requirements.

This Joper's flame is in desperate need of tuning.

5

Preparation And Consistency

Consistent results

Achieving perfectly consistent roasting is impossible with today's technology. Even if you control the ambient roastery temperature and the green-coffee temperature, implement an effective *between-batch protocol*, and employ optimal data-logging equipment, you'll still fail to replicate roasts perfectly. As an industry, we're nowhere near the point where even the best roasters replicate roasts well enough to regularly fool a skilled *cupper*.

Inconsistency is the number one reason I hesitate when people ask me from whom they should buy roasted coffee. Even the best roasters I know find it difficult to replicate their best roasts.

While some roasting inconsistency is caused by factors difficult to control, the more variables you manage to control or eliminate, the more repeatable your roasts will be. Here are some strategies to help you improve repeatability.

Green-coffee temperature

Perhaps the easiest way to improve roast repeatability is to stabilize green-coffee temperature. Always charging with green of a constant temperature makes roasting results far more consistent. In fact, if your green-coffee temperature varies even a little from day to day, it's impossible to replicate roasts. True, your *Cropster* curves may look identical, but given that bean-temperature curves reflect only surface temperatures, two identical Cropster curves won't produce the same flavor if the core bean temperatures were different at charge.

It may be impractical to maintain a constant ambient temperature in a large roastery, but it's worth putting some effort into preventing temperature swings. At the very least, I recommend not allowing ambient temperature to drop below 60°F (16°C) or above 80°F (27°C). If necessary, move the roasting machine to a smaller space that's easier to climate-control than a larger warehouse.

Warming up a roaster

Given that the first batch of the day is difficult to predict or manage, many roasters seem to have given up trying to master it. Most seem to carelessly roast decaf or some other less-important coffee as the first batch. While it's sensible to roast a low-priority coffee as the first batch of the day, there is no excuse for not dialing in that batch as well as possible. Simply put, the better one roasts the first batch, the easier it will be to roast the next batch well, and so on.

It's not possible to prescribe a detailed, universal warm-up or between-batch protocol for all machines. I recommend the procedure in the box to the right as a starting point for an effective warm-up. Try it and adjust as needed. If the warm-up procedure is successful, the first batch of the day will behave nearly identically to later batches of the same coffee. If the warm-up was not hot enough or long enough, the first batch's curve will begin sluggishly and have a low *turning point*. If the warm-up was too long or too hot, the first roast will be quicker than usual out of the gate, with a high turning point.

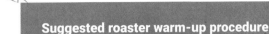

Suggested roaster warm-up procedure

1. Bring the BT up to charge temp + 40°F (20°C) using medium–high gas
2. Idle at charge + 40°F (20°C) for 25–30 minutes (add 10–20 minutes on cold days)
3. Lower the gas so the BT drops to charge + 10°F (5°C) in approximately 5–10 minutes
4. Perform a between-batch protocol (BBP)
5. Charge

Here are some recommendations for designing a warm-up procedure:
- The probe readings should be hotter than the nominal charge temperature for

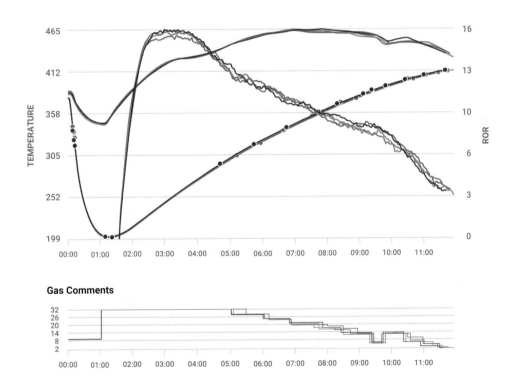

Adjust your warm-up procedure daily until your first few curves track each other at least as closely as these do.

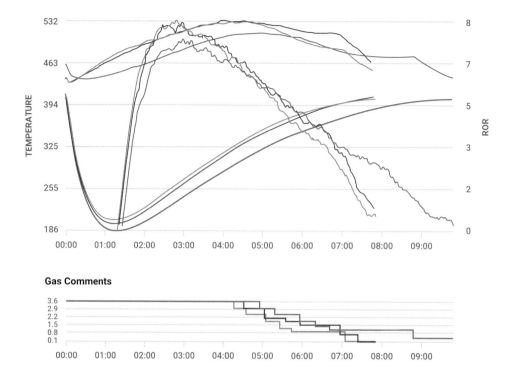

Gas Comments

These three batches roasted at very different speeds because the roasting machine was not adequately warmed up before the first batch (blue curve).

the majority of the warm-up. If one simply warms up to—but not above—the charge temperature, it will take an excessively long time for the machine's *thermal energy* to rise to the target equilibrium thermal energy.

- Before charging the first batch, consider enacting a between-batch protocol as if you had just completed a roast. Depending on the sufficiency of the warm-up, you may need a modified BBP with a higher bottoming temperature (for example, bottoming at 10°F / 5°C below charge rather than 20°F / 10°C below charge).

Managing roastery temperature in winter

For readers who roast in areas where the temperature drops to freezing at night, it may be worth investing in a modified chimney, both to lower heating costs and to improve roasting consistency. A few years ago, I woke up early in Colorado to roast with a new client. The previous night had been by far the coldest so far that year. When we arrived at the café to roast, the café's ambient temperature was a comfortable 20°C (68°F), but the interior of the roaster was nearly freezing. The warm-up took 45 minutes longer than usual, and the first batch still wasn't as good as we had hoped it would be.

That day I began thinking about how to modify roasting chimneys to prevent cold overnight temperatures from affecting roasting and warming up. Since then,

I've had clients install two different solutions: one is a leak-proof slide gate that they close overnight to prevent cold outside air from entering the roastery. The other is a removable section of chimney they cap when not in use. Each solution is a good investment in areas where cold overnight air may increase the heating bill as well as the time and energy required to warm up the roaster.

Between-batch protocol (BBP)

The purpose of a BBP is to reset a roasting machine's thermal energy between batches. With an effective BBP, one can roast numerous consecutive batches of a coffee using identical gas settings to replicate roast curves

Suggested between-batch protocols

Between-Batch Protocol I (More Common):
- Set gas to zero, drop batch, close door.
- Drift down with zero or low gas until the BT reaches the exact chosen bottoming temperature (perhaps 40°F / 20°C below charge). Drifting down should take 2:30–4:00.
- At the bottoming temperature, use low-to-medium gas to rise to the charge temperature in 1:30.
- Charge as soon as the charge temperature is reached.

Between-Batch Protocol II (Less Common):
- Set gas to zero, drop batch, close door.
- Use low-to-medium gas until the BT reads 20°F (10°C) above charge temperature.
- Set gas off or to a very low setting such that the BT reading drifts down to the charge temperature in 1:30–2:30.
- Charge as soon as the charge temperature is reached.

and cupping results nearly perfectly. In my experience, most roasters' batches get faster as a roast day progresses, which means they need to improve their BBPs.

Almost all roasters should use Protocol I; users of some rare machines may benefit from Protocol II. Examples of machines requiring Protocol II are large machines that retain heat too efficiently to drop 40°F (20°C) below charge temperature in less than 6 minutes and machines that don't allow the operator to turn off the gas fully between batches.

Mastering repeatability

Once a roaster has fine-tuned his warm-up and BBP, his bean curves should "trace" each other perfectly when plotted together on a graph. Here is a typical example, from one of my clients, of excellent repeatability across fourteen consecutive roasts:

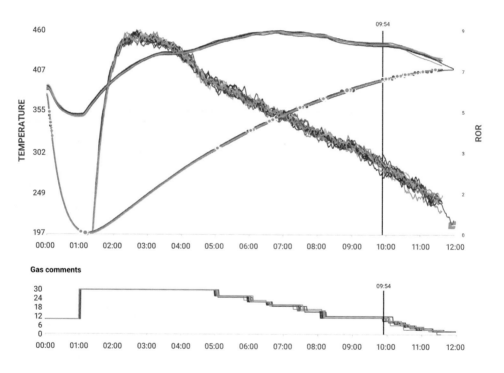

This graph depicts fifteen consecutive batches. I'm proud to say this client achieves this level of repeatability every day.

Planning a roast day

To make repeatability as easy as possible, one would choose to always roast only one batch size and to roast every batch to the same degree. However, the practicalities of business often demand one use different batch sizes and degrees of roast. If possible, I strongly recommend roasters resist attempting to master more than two batch sizes, as one is hard enough! If one must roast a variety of coffees, batch sizes, and roast degrees, plan a roast day with these priorities in mind:

- Roast your least important coffees first.
- Roast smaller batches before larger batches.
- Roast lighter batches before darker batches.
- Organize batches to avoid making more than one change in batch size during a roasting session.

When switching between batch sizes, one needs to implement a special BBP to reset the machine's thermal energy. When shifting from smaller batches to larger batches, the BBP may include idling at a temperature above charge for several minutes before implementing a more standard BBP. When shifting to smaller batches, the BBP may involve bottoming at a much lower temperature than usual before heating up to the charge temperature. Mastering this special BBP is perhaps the most difficult task in roasting.

6

Setting Reasonable Parameters

This may surprise readers, but it's difficult to "taste" roast time, airflow, drum speed, or numerous other roasting variables if they are set to reasonable levels. Sure, if you roast two batches and change any one of those variables during the second batch, the roasts will taste different. But you may not be tasting the *direct* effect of the variable; it's more likely you're tasting the variable's effect on the bean-temperature and ROR curves.

The key word in the last paragraph is "reasonable." Unreasonable values, such as a 6-minute roast of a full batch, a drum rpm of 35 in a 12-kg roaster, or airflow set too low to remove smoke and chaff, will yield identifiable roast defects. Respectively, those three mistakes will produce underdevelopment, roasty (and probably *baked*) flavors, and smoky coffee. A trained palate has a chance of guessing what went wrong in those roasts.

Roasting is complex. Changing any one variable always triggers a chain reaction that alters several other variables; this makes it nearly impossible to use a scientific method to test the effects of single variables, reasonably adjusted, on roast quality. The more effective approach to roast experimentation is to roast thousands of batches and to analyze what parameters resulted in successful roasts or certain defects most often. Think of it as a "big data"–inspired version of roasting experimentation. This approach asks you to roast hundreds or thousands of batches before becoming cautiously confident about the relationship between a roast parameter and the resulting flavor. There are no shortcuts.

The next few chapters contain insights I have gained from two decades of roasting and big data–inspired analysis. I'll provide reasonable ranges, or "best practices" for roast parameters to offer the greatest chance of success. It will be up to the reader to adapt the best practices to their own machines and coffees.

Batch size

As I discussed in *The Coffee Roaster's Companion*, a roasting machine's optimal batch size is almost always smaller than its stated capacity. The typical 12-kg roaster can rarely roast more than 8–9 kilograms of green coffee without compromising quality. Many years ago I devised a formula that has served me well on hundreds of roasting machines:

> **One pound of green coffee requires approximately 5,000 BTU/hour of rated burner output for optimal roasting. (In metric terms, 1 kilogram of green coffee requires 11,600 kj/hour of burner capacity.)**

For example, if a roasting machine's rated burner output is 100,000 BTU/hour (105,500 kj/hour), that implies one should roast no more than 20 lb (9 kg) per batch. Note that 20 lb is the maximum recommended batch size, not the optimal batch size. Smaller batches will, on average, taste better. But roasting of batches larger than 20 lb may noticeably compromise quality.

Many roasting-machine salespeople will dispute these facts. They routinely claim their machines can roast full batches—which is true, but not without compromising quality. That should not surprise the reader, as salespeople are biased and incentivized to overstate the capabilities of the machines they sell. So please ignore the claims and simply ask about the burner's rated power output. It's a better estimate of a machine's true capacity. I also recommend surveying users of a machine to find out their average batch sizes, roast times, and number of batches per hour.

Charge temperature

Charge temperature is not as important as the BBP that precedes charging. For example, if one idles at 440°F (227°C) for 5 minutes before charging at 410°F (210°C), the machine's thermal energy will be much greater than if one charges at 410°F (210°C) after idling at 350°F (177°C) for 5 minutes between batches.

MACHINE SIZE	CHARGE TEMPERATURE
500 g–1 kg	350°F–380°F (175°C–190°C)
6 kg	360°F–390°F (185°C–200°C)
12 kg–20 kg	380°F–410°F (195°C–210°C)
30 kg	390°F–420°F (200°C–215°C)

That said, one must choose a charge temperature, and assuming that one's BBP approximates the one I recommend in Chapter 5, I'll propose the following reasonable charge-temperature ranges. Feel free to be liberal with these suggestions, as they do not account for all possible variations in batch size, machine power, or drum design. They are merely offered as a starting point.

Roast time

Ideal roast time depends on, among other things, machine capacity and the ratio of batch size to burner output. Most pros know this intuitively, as they have cupped fantastic 7-minute batches from *sample roasters* but would not attempt a 7-minute roast in a relatively full production roaster.

For example, if a 12-kg machine's maximum burner output is 100,000 BTU per hour (105,500 kj/hour), I'd aim to roast 20 lb (9 kg) in approximately 12–13 minutes. At "half capacity" (relative to burner power), I would roast 10-lb (4.5-kg) batches in 8–10 minutes. These recommendations are rough estimates, and ideal roast times will vary depending on the machine, bean type, and other factors. For example, optimal roast times are shorter for drums less likely to cause conductive damage to beans.

Roast time's effect on flavor is difficult to wrap one's head around. On the one hand, many of us can cup a production roast and sense it was roasted too quickly. On the other hand, a given roast time does not have an obvious signature flavor . . . for example, a 6:00 light roast of 100 g in a sample roaster may taste delicious and well developed, while a 10-kg batch of the same coffee roasted in 6:00 on a Probat P12 will almost certainly be underdeveloped and possibly scorched. Therefore, one cannot generalize about the flavor of 6-minute roasts.

For readers just wanting the bottom line . . . if you're roasting batch sizes of between 50% and 70% of capacity, consider 10:00–12:00 to be your target range for most batches. If you need to use 100% gas for several minutes in order to keep batch duration below 12:00, consider roasting smaller batches.

7

Reading Roast Curves

The bean-temperature probe (aka bean probe) is in contact with the bean pile during a roast and generates the bean-temperature curve (aka bean curve). The bean probe's readout approximates the local surface temperature of the bean pile, but it is also influenced by its contact with the hot air surrounding the beans. The probe's own mass creates *thermal lag*, which makes the bean-temperature data inaccurate, especially when the bean temperature changes rapidly during the first few minutes of a roast. The combined influence of the air temperature and the probe's thermal lag affect how accurately the probe's readings reflect the actual surface temperature of the bean pile.

A typical bean curve drops from the high temperature of the charge down to the turn, rises rapidly at first, and then decelerates during the rest of the roast. The descending curve before the turn is not an accurate indication of the bean temperature; it is an artifact of the probe's thermal lag. After all, if the beans were 70°F (21°C) at charge, an accurate bean curve would begin at 70°F (21°C) and rise rapidly from there.

The ROR curve is the *derivative* of the bean curve, or the rate of change of the bean temperatures per unit of time. The slope and shape of an ROR curve depend on the speed of the bean probe as well as on several roast parameters, such as batch size, gas settings, and charge temperature. The slope and shape of an ROR offer insight into the roast's effect on cup quality.

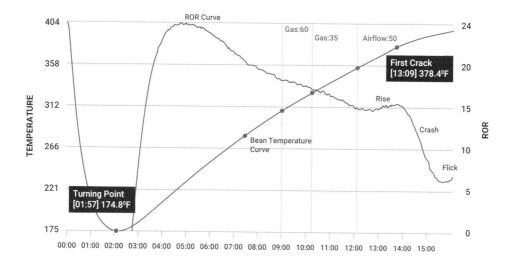

The unmanaged roast

The curve graphed above reflects many elements of a poor roast, including a rising ROR (or hump) before first crack, an ROR crash after first crack, and a *flick*, or rise in the ROR after the crash. I refer to such a roast as "unmanaged" because it demonstrates a pattern typical of roasts on older machines that offer poor controls (such as only two or three available gas settings) and roasts managed without data-logging software. Achieving smooth ROR curves require skill. Curves like the one above will often occur naturally if one roasts batches passively or reactively.

If the ROR rises or forms a hump near the beginning of first crack, it may impart a "roasty" flavor in the cup. If the ROR crashes or declines rapidly, usually just after first crack begins (or occasionally later), the coffee may taste baked. An upturn, or flick, in the ROR at the end of a roast will cause roasty flavor.

Baked roasts

As roasters have adopted data-logging software and better temperature probes, roast curves have become smoother and more consistent. Versions of the unmanaged roast were likely the dominant curve shapes for decades. Since publication of *The Coffee Roaster's Companion*, an ever-increasing number of roasters have focused on achieving smoothly declining RORs.

Perhaps the most common and most difficult to avoid roast defect is the ROR crash. An ROR crash is a near-vertical drop in the ROR curve, usually occurring during the early moments of first crack. No particular angle or slope defines an ROR crash, and none can, because probe speed and software smoothing influence curve shape. For a given bean probe, the angle of an ROR's downturn, aka its "degree of crash," as well as its timing determine how baked a roast will taste.

Baking a roast decreases its sweetness and fruity acidity and replaces those characteristics with flat, hollow flavors reminiscent of straw or cardboard. I speculate that prior to the popular adoption of data-logging software, almost all roasts

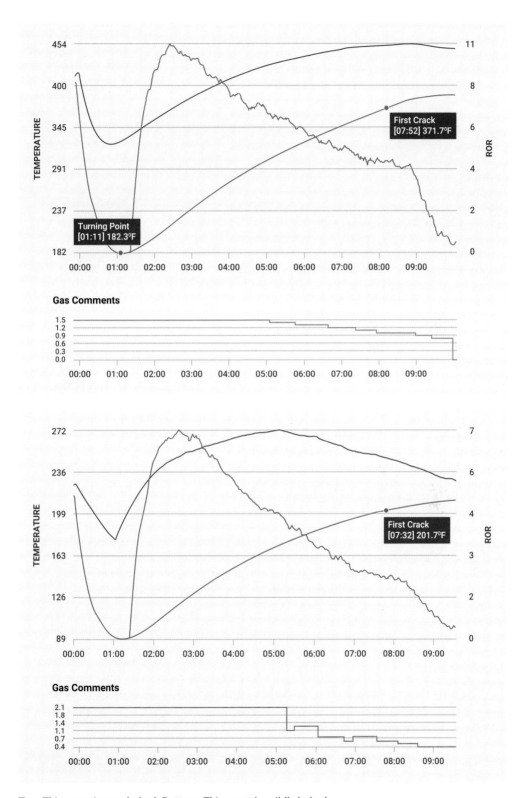

Top: This roast is very baked. **Bottom:** This roast is mildly baked.

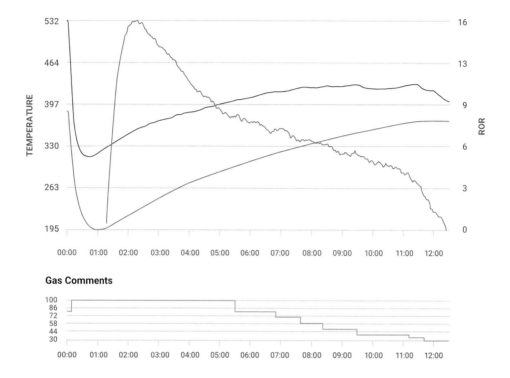

Gas Comments

The late, soft crash makes it difficult to predict how baked this roast will taste.

resembled versions of the unmanaged roast, meaning that they were baked as well as roasty. In recent years, with the help of software and better probes, roasters and consumers have gradually come to embrace lighter, sweeter, less-baked coffee. I still meet the odd professional who argues that crashed RORs do not cause baking or reduce coffee's sweetness, but those meetings are rarer each year.

The one possible departure from the rule that an ROR crash bakes coffee is what I call the "Nordic exception." Many roasters from the Nordic countries prefer to roast batches lightly and quickly, with relatively high, flat RORs that crash gently just before discharge of the beans. If an ROR crash is late enough or gentle enough, as it sometimes is in such roasts, the crash doesn't seem to cause the beans to taste as baked as the graph would imply. I'll speculate that a very late crash doesn't impart as much baked flavor to the coffee because the crash did not have enough time to alter the development of deeper layers in the coffee beans.

The flick

The flick is a rise in the ROR at the end of a roast. A flick usually follows a crash, but it may occur without a curve having crashed first. Contrary to popular belief, a flick may occur despite the gas setting being low or off. As noted, a flick adds a layer of roasty flavor to a batch; the larger the flick, the greater the effect. Remember to always consider the probe speed and software settings when evaluating the

Coffee Roasting: Best Practices

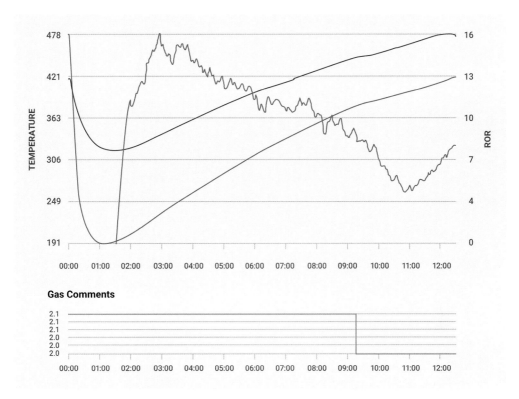

This coffee will taste roasty, even if it was dropped at a light color. Note that the flick occurred despite the very low gas setting.

size of a flick. When the probe is slow and the data are smoothed, the flick will look smaller or may no longer look like a flick. The best way to avoid a flick is to use the recommendations in Chapter 10 on how to manage gas settings after first crack.

The smoothly declining ROR

The best roasts I've tasted always had a smoothly declining ROR. The superiority of smoothly declining RORs has been controversial, though less so over time. In my experience, roasters almost always become converts to smooth RORs after they have learned to masterfully replicate them. Until a roaster has produced and tasted hundreds of batches with smoothly declining RORs, he does not have enough experience to judge their merits.

Almost every client I have ever worked with has become convinced of the benefit of smoothly declining RORs. Some came to favor smooth RORs rapidly, and some took months to convince.

I have tasted enjoyable coffee from roasts that lacked smoothly declining RORs. However, those roasts were always of exceptional green coffee that managed to be tasty despite subpar roasting, and in every case wherein I had the opportunity to influence future batches of the same coffee, the best-tasting batches were the ones

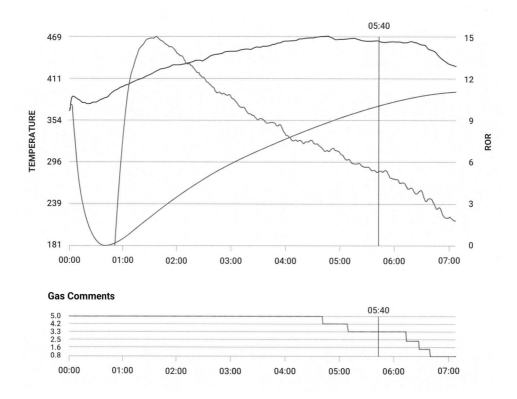

Gas Comments

This curve looks promising but does not tell us the degree of roast development.

with the smoothest ROR slopes. It's important to remember that if a coffee tastes great, it doesn't mean it couldn't have been better.

While a smoothly declining ROR is possibly a prerequisite for a stellar roast, it is not a guarantee of a successful roast; one cannot know whether a batch is well developed merely by looking at its bean-temperature and ROR curves. Roast-curve data reflect bean-surface-temperature measurements only, and that does not tell us much about inner-bean temperatures or development. For example, we can see that the roast above is not baked, and it likely isn't unduly roasty, but we don't know if it is adequately developed. As of now, there is no clear way to deduce underdevelopment from bean-temperature data.

Development time ratio (DTR): what it means, and what it doesn't

When I wrote *The Coffee Roaster's Companion*, I introduced the original idea of thinking of development time as a ratio of total roast time. Prior to publication, it was standard for roasters to discuss development time without reference to total roast time. In isolation, knowing that a roast's development time is 1:30, for example, is rather meaningless. Thinking in terms of *development time ratio (DTR)* provides a better sense of whether a roast was in balance. The shape and proportions of a bean curve (or, more practically, its ROR curve) are better predictors of flavor and development than are the absolute times a roast spent in various phases.

In *The Coffee Roaster's Companion*, I recommended a DTR range of 20%–25%. That recommendation generated a fair amount of controversy over the years. What few of the critics grasped was that *CRC* was written for all roasters, not just the 1% of roasters who prefer extremely light, Nordic-style roasts. While I have nothing against such light roasts and personally prefer them, the 20%–25% advice has benefitted the vast majority of roasters who, prior to reading *CRC*, had never thought in terms of DTR and had not been trying to smooth their ROR curves. Those roasters needed some reasonable, tangible roast-curve targets. For the vast majority of the world's roasters, achieving a steadily declining ROR and a 20%–25% DTR were revolutionary ideas that improved their average roast quality.

I recommend that roasters view DTR as an indicator of a balanced roast, and only that. Please don't drop roasts exclusively based on DTR, as roast color is a better indicator of a roast's completion. If a batch has not reached your desired roast color but it has reached 25% DTR, don't sweat it; just keep roasting until you reach the desired roast color or bean temperature. If you're dropping batches mid-first crack and your DTRs are above 25%, or if you drop roasts during second crack and DTRs are near 20%, you may want to consider rebalancing your heat application. But please don't overreact, in the moment, to an undesired DTR. Instead, drop the roast at the desired color and later analyze what went wrong.

8

How Probe Speed and Location Influence Curves

Art vs. science

Too often I hear a refrain from roasters that goes something like this: "My coffee tastes great and my customers love it, so why should I care about software and curves?" As compelling as that argument may seem, it's not worth much. Other than the obvious argument that we should always strive to improve our coffee and become expert in our craft, one should not trust roasters' (biased) opinions of their

own coffee. One cannot master the craft of roasting without understanding and mastering the skill of interpreting roast curves. For those who disagree, consider that the quality of specialty roasting was stagnant for decades prior to the widespread use of data-logging software, and it improved rapidly thereafter.

Prior to using data-logging software, most roasters were satisfied using a spreadsheet to track gas settings, roast time, final bean temperature, and perhaps the beginning of first crack. A scant few diligent roasters tracked bean temperature values by hand, every minute of every batch. Like today's roasters, roasters back then also thought highly of their quality and consistency, but when data-logging software came into use, those old results and spreadsheets suddenly looked erratic and amateur.

Mining roast data and comparing the data to cupping results is the most efficient and effective way to learn and improve. Data-obsessed roasters can improve their craft at startling rates, much faster than roasters were ever able to before the advent of data-logging software.

Data interpretation

Skillful interpretation of roast data is difficult. Before attempting to interpret roast data, it's important to understand how probe speed and software settings affect the accuracy and shapes of roast curves. Probes have their own mass that slows and smooths readings due to thermal lag. Software such as Cropster and *Artisan* create ROR curves from these lagged temperature readings by averaging them over a chosen time interval (15 seconds is typical), further smoothing the data. In other words, points on bean-temperature curves and ROR curves are not real-time readings; instead, they represent the smoothed and delayed results of real-time readings. When we roast, we are always viewing data from the past.

The trick is to use the optimal amount of smoothing for your needs. Inadequate smoothing leads to excessive noise, making data patterns more difficult to notice. Excessive smoothing makes data unnecessarily slow and inaccurate. Once you have properly adjusted the smoothing, you can successfully analyze curves for relevant patterns (humps, crashes, flicks, etc.) that correlate with cup qualities.

Optimal probe size

As a general rule, thinner and lighter probes are more responsive and produce less lag but more noise. I recommend using an *ungrounded* J- or K-type thermocouple

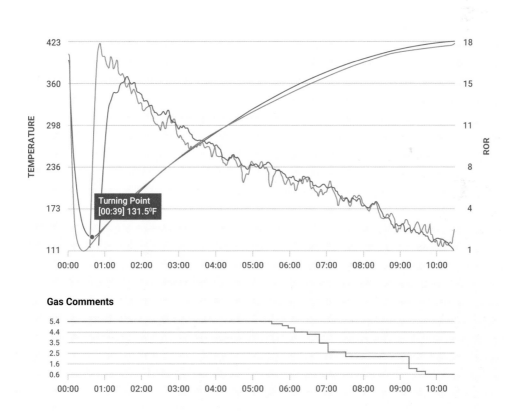

This roast's ROR curves were created by two thin thermocouples, sizes 1 mm (yellow) and 3 mm (blue), respectively. In this case, the 1-mm thermocouple created excessive noise, and the ROR from the 3-mm is easier to read. Not all 1-mm probes will be so noisy, but I offer this graph as an example of acceptable noise versus excessive noise.

or RTD probe of approximately 3 mm in diameter. Smaller probes can be useful, though most roasters will find that data from 3-mm probes offer a good balance of accuracy and noise.

Probe speed and ROR curve shape

When I refer to a "smoothly declining ROR" I'm referring to an ROR with a relatively constant slope, but not necessarily a straight line. There can be no universal, ideal slope for all roasting machines or coffees because the speed of the bean probe affects a curve's shape and slope. Slower probes produce humped ROR curves, while very fast probes yield straight-to-slumped RORs. The three graphs on these two pages illustrate the effects of probe speed on ROR curve shape and noise.

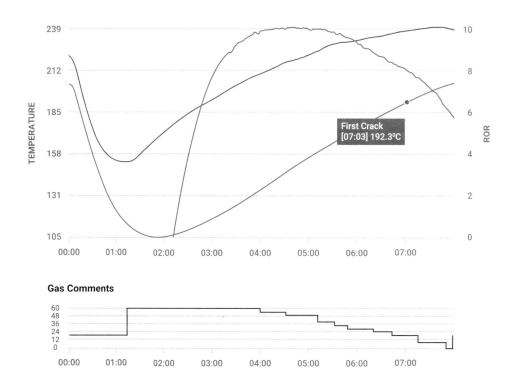

Note how the ROR from the slow probe arcs throughout the roast.

The important takeaway here is that one cannot evaluate a roast curve without considering the responsiveness of the probe involved. The easiest way to estimate relative probe speed is to look at the timing of the turn—the earlier the turn, the faster the probe, all else being equal.

Trends vs. events

When analyzing ROR curves, I am sometimes interested in seeing trends in the data and sometimes interested in momentary events. An example of a trend would be a long, flat stretch in an ROR curve before first crack, while an event

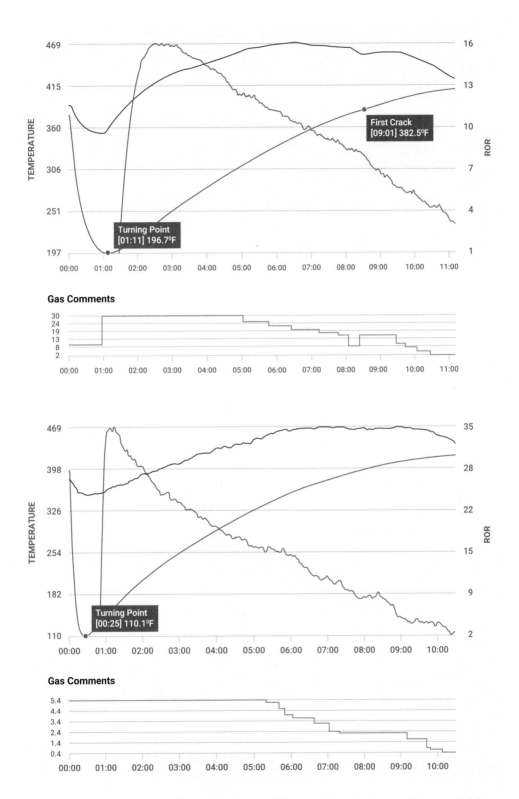

Gas Comments

Gas Comments

Top: The 3-mm probe's ROR is nearly straight. **Bottom:** The curve from the 1-mm probe sags slightly.

would be the moment an ROR curve stops dropping and begins to flick.

To see trends clearly, it's usually best to increase the *ROR interval* (in Cropster) or *delta span* (in Artisan) to smooth a curve and decrease its noise. In the graph below, the ROR interval is set to 30 seconds, making it easy to discern trends, such as the flattening of the ROR between 6:00 and 7:00, the small hump near 7:30, and the subsequent crash.

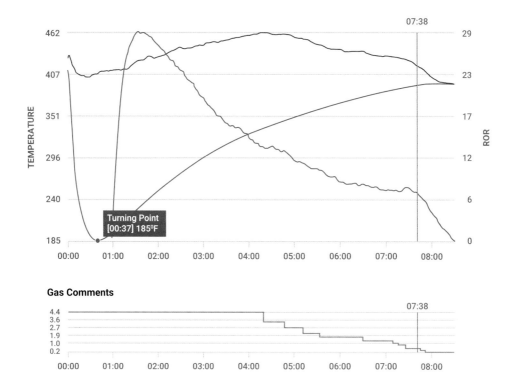

To smooth the hump and the crash, I recommend using a method called the *gas dip* (see Chapter 11). Executing the gas dip well requires knowing precisely when the crash (an event) began. To see the crash timing more clearly, I have chosen to set the ROR interval in the curve on the following page to 10 seconds (the shortest interval offered by Cropster). While that created a lot of noise in the data, it also shifted the perceived beginning of the crash to 7:27 from 7:38. That 11-second difference is critical to success when a roaster uses the gas dip.

Coffee Roasting: Best Practices

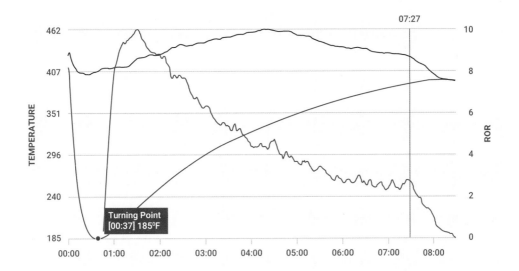

Gas Comments

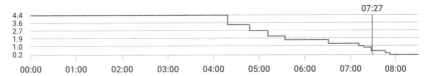

9

Airflow Management

Dampers vs. variable-speed fans

Roasting machines offer two airflow-control mechanisms: adjustable *dampers* and variable-speed fans. A damper is a rather crude means of affecting the airflow within a narrow range. If your machine has only a damper, it's usually best to "set it and forget it" because it may be too clunky and imprecise (or too hot!) to adjust with consistency and precision during roasts. To get a sense of where to set the damper, use the cigarette-lighter test discussed in Chapter 4, roast a few test batches, make small adjustments as needed, and then leave the damper as-is for a few weeks.

Relative to a damper, adjustable fans offer more precision, better repeatability, and a wider range of airflow settings. All suggestions below assume the use of a variable-speed fan.

No airflow adjustments required

We've all tasted great roasts from old Probat UG machines that offered little in the way of airflow adjustment. Experience with those machines and others proves that adjusting airflow mid-roast is not necessary to produce stellar coffee.

The damper on a Probat P12

One or more adjustments on drum roasters

I recommend making all airflow changes at least 2 minutes before first crack. Increasing the fan too close to first crack increases the risk that the ROR becomes flat or goes up, and it often increases the risk of a crash. (More on this in Chapter 10.)

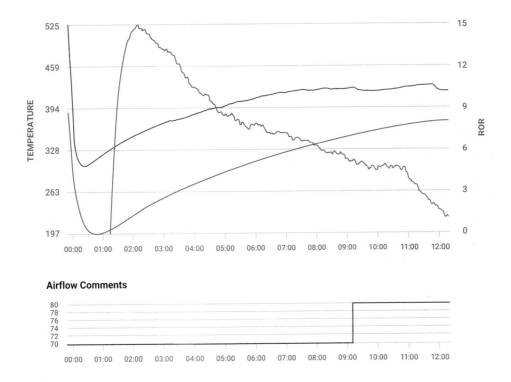

Airflow Comments

The roaster increased the airflow too close to the beginning of first crack, causing the ROR to flatten and ultimately crash.

How a fan adjustment affects a roast curve depends on the timing and magnitude of the adjustment, the batch size, the machine's thermal energy, and other factors. The usual immediate impact of an increase in airflow is a temporary acceleration of a roast—for several seconds the ROR may either go up, or else it may go down more slowly—likely because the additional airflow strips stored heat from the machine's surfaces. To help maintain smoother ROR curves when adjusting airflow, I recommend increasing the fan setting shortly after lowering the gas. In other words, lower the gas, wait 2 or 3 seconds, and then increase the fan setting.

Machines requiring airflow management

It is usually beneficial to adjust airflow during a roast when using an underpowered classic-drum roaster or when overloading a machine relative to its burner power. In underpowered drum roasters, restricting airflow during the first few minutes of a batch traps heat in the machine, which speeds up otherwise sluggish roasts.
When roasting on *electric machines* and indirectly heated drum roasters, charge with low airflow and medium-to-high burner power and progressively lower the burner setting and increase the airflow throughout a roast. This strategy manages release of the machine's stored energy and improves control late in roasts.

10

Basic Gas Management

While there are many approaches to timing gas settings, the following simple methods should work on all machines. This is a purely practical "how-to" chapter; the following chapters will discuss the reasons behind these methods, as well as some more advanced techniques.

Charge with high gas, and lower the gas stepwise as the batch progresses

Charging a mass of cold beans into a roaster dramatically lowers the machine's thermal energy and the air temperature within the drum. Using a high gas setting during the early stages of a roast helps to bring the roasting environment up to reasonable roasting temperatures.

This is probably the most common gas-management system in roasting: charge with a high gas setting, wait until the bean temperature is roughly 300°F (150°C),

Lower gas power

Apply this method to the electric roasters? (handwritten)

An example of standard gas settings for a roast

Charge at 390°F (199°C) with a 70% capacity batch:

- Gas 95% at charge
- Lower gas to 75% at BT (bean temperature) 295°F (146°C)
- Gas 60% at BT 325°F (163°C)
- Gas 45% at BT 340°F (171°C)
- Gas 30% at BT 360°F (182°C)
- Gas 20% at BT 372°F (189°C)
- First crack
- Gas 15% at 12% DTR*
- Gas 10% at 14% DTR
- Gas 5% at 16% DTR

* Later in this chapter I discuss the timing of gas settings after first crack.

and then <u>lower the gas several times before first crack</u> and a few more times after first crack. The curve below is an example of this approach; optimal gas settings will vary for different machines and situations.

The soak

The *soak* is an alternative way to manage the first few minutes of a roast. To soak is simply to charge with a low gas setting (or perhaps no gas) and to raise the gas to its peak setting within the first 2 minutes of the batch. If you choose to soak, I recommend using 20% gas for 1 minute as a starting point.

While the soak may be applied to any batch on any machine, I prefer to soak in only these two situations:

- Roasting on small (smaller than

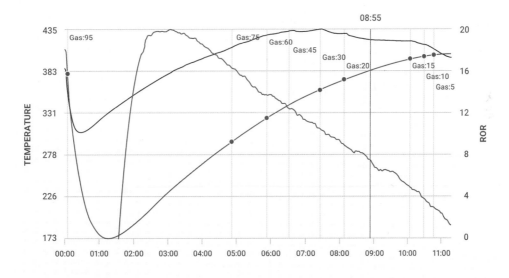

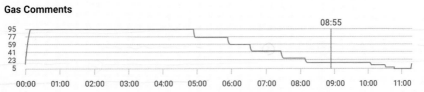

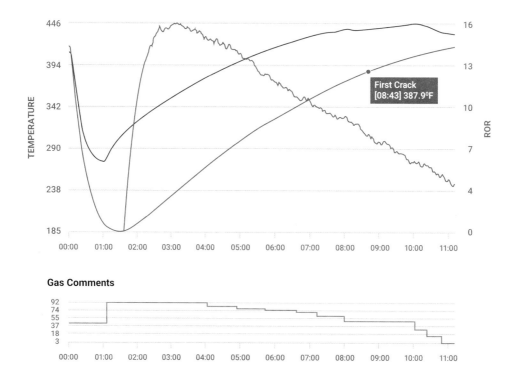

Gas Comments

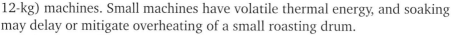

There is no standard gas setting or duration for the soak. The roaster here chose to soak at 40% gas for 1 minute.

12-kg) machines. Small machines have volatile thermal energy, and soaking may delay or mitigate overheating of a small roasting drum.

• Roasting on machines resistant to cooling between batches. The soak is helpful when a machine is difficult to cool between batches due to heavy insulation or inadequate airflow.

Basic ROR management approaching first crack

Let's say a roaster charged a batch without the soak and steadily lowered the gas after BT 300°F (150°C). Most likely, the ROR dropped smoothly, but as the roast approached first crack, the roaster knew ROR management was about to get trickier. A good rule of thumb is to substantially lower the gas about 40–45 seconds before you anticipate the beginning of first crack. Removing just the right amount of gas at that time gives you a good chance of maintaining a smoothly declining ROR just before and after the beginning of first crack. However, determining that "just right" amount of gas may require some trial and error. The following scenarios assume the airflow setting was appropriate and was not increased in the 2 minutes preceding first crack.

• If the ROR flattens or rises, and then crashes, the gas was too high.

• If the ROR declines steadily before first crack and *stalls* or flatlines during first crack, the gas was too low.

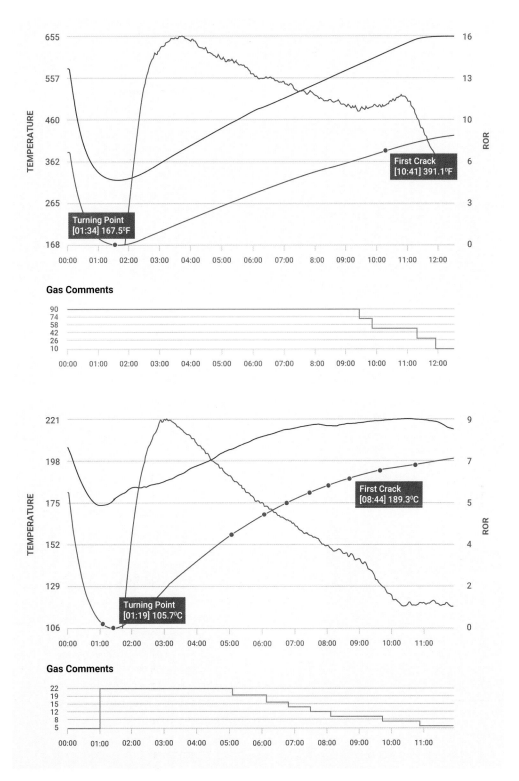

Top: This roast's gas setting was much too high leading up to first crack. **Bottom:** The roaster lowered the gas too much in the middle stages of the batch, causing the low, flat ROR after first crack.

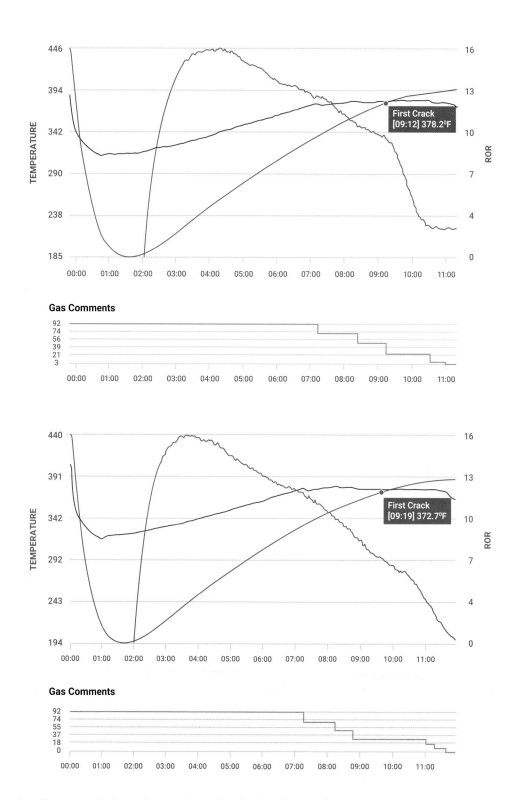

Top: The roaster likely used too much gas heading into first crack. **Bottom:** Using lower gas settings before first crack fixed the crash.

Fixing "soft" ROR crashes

The top graph on the opposite page is an example of a curve with a soft ROR crash. To smooth a soft crash with a declining ROR heading into the crash, my first choice would be to lower the mid-roast gas settings more aggressively.

Fixing "hard" ROR crashes

One probably cannot smooth the ROR crash in the graph below merely by lowering the gas settings mid-roast. I consider this a "hard" ROR crash because the turndown in the ROR curve was abrupt and almost 90 degrees, and the roaster had already chosen a very low gas setting well before the crash. I recommend using the gas dip (Chapter 11) to fix hard ROR crashes.

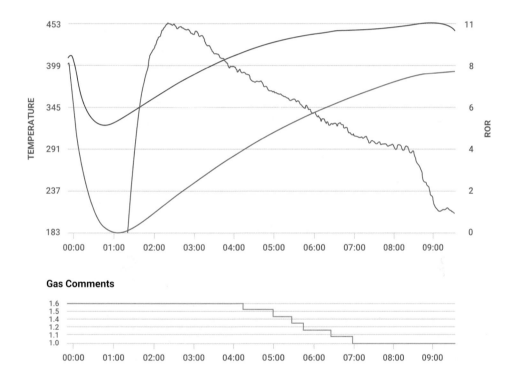

Gas Comments

Adjusting the gas after first crack

I recommend timing your gas adjustments based on bean temperature prior to first crack and based on DTR after first crack. Because the bean temperature changes slowly, and often unpredictably after first crack, bean temperature is a poor indicator of when to change the gas. DTR, on the other hand, is an excellent predictor of crashes and flicks and how to prevent them.

A standard pattern of gas changes after first crack may look like this:
- Cut gas in half at 12% DTR
- Cut gas in half again at 14% DTR
- Cut gas in half again at 16% DTR, or possibly turn off gas

Inlet temperature

Inlet temperature (IT) is the temperature of the hot air as it enters the roasting drum from the burner. Most roasters don't measure inlet temperature, but it is a useful tool for predicting and controlling roast curves. Some larger roasting machines use preprogrammed inlet temperatures, rather than gas settings, to manage roasts.

While gas settings are the "inputs" roasters use to adjust burner temperatures, the inlet temperature is the "output" of that effort, and it more directly reflects what beans experience during a roast. Inlet temperature is arguably more relevant than gas setting.

Subjectively, I consider gas settings simpler and more intuitive to manage, but inlet temperature settings offer a potentially more effective way to control roasts. While I won't directly address how to program inlet temperatures, I recommend roasters track the IT curve, even if they manage roasts purely by adjusting gas settings.

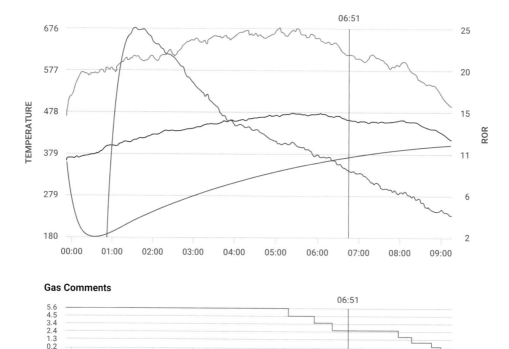

The jagged yellow curve at the top of the graph indicates the inlet temperature.

11

The Phases of Moisture Release and the Gas Dip

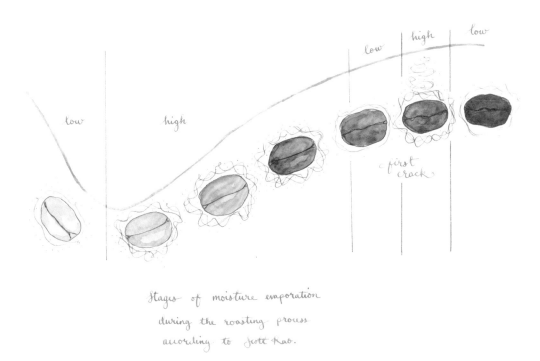

low   high   low   high   low

first
crack

Stages of moisture evaporation
during the roasting process
according to Scott Rao.

Green coffee contains approximately 8%–12% moisture by weight. Chemical reactions during roasting create water and also release it from the beans, leaving beans with approximately 1.5%–2.5% moisture content after roasting. In *Espresso Coffee: The Science of Quality*, Illy describes an "evaporative front" of cool moisture created by the release of water vapor from beans. Much as perspiration may evaporate off our skin during a run on a hot summer day, cooling us, moisture release during roasting causes *evaporative cooling* of bean surfaces. The front of moisture emanating from beans inhibits transfer of heat into them during roasting; therefore, the more moisture beans release during a roast, the more heat one must apply to cook the beans to a given degree.

ROR. He should generally apply more gas during phases when the beans release more moisture and apply less gas when moisture release slows.

There is one exception: although moisture release accelerates and peaks during first crack, a roaster should never rely on a large increase in gas setting to prevent an ROR crash. Raising the gas may produce a smooth curve, but the coffee will likely taste "roasty" and less delicate.

> A roaster should never rely on a large increase in gas setting to prevent an ROR crash.

During Phase 3, just before first crack, moisture release slows and possibly stops. As noted in Chapter 10, it's a good strategy to lower the gas substantially 40–45 seconds before first crack begins. This strategy is adequate when roasting a coffee not prone to a hard ROR crash because a single, well-chosen gas setting will prevent the ROR from flattening or rising before first crack, and it will supply enough energy to prevent an ROR crash after first crack.

If a coffee's ROR crashes despite your best efforts during Phase 3, I recommend an advanced method called the gas dip.

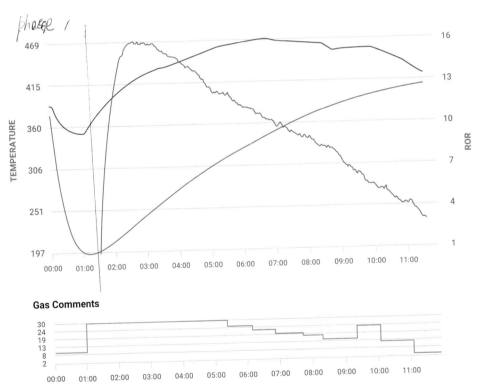

Raising the gas may produce an attractive curve, but the coffee will taste roasty.

The basics of the gas dip

To execute the gas dip, the roaster decreases the gas by 50% for 20 seconds and then, approximately 15 seconds before the anticipated ROR crash, brings the gas back up to its pre-dip level.

The gas dip method

The gas dip method is especially useful when other methods fail to prevent an ROR from crashing. The gas dip is the only time I recommend increasing the gas late in a roast. If you attempt the gas dip, please follow the prescribed method exactly. It is a high-risk, high-return method that can easily ruin a roast, so I recommend using the gas dip only with coffees prone to crashing hard, as there will be little to lose.

On this page and the next are two consecutive batches of a Rwandan coffee. In the first batch the ROR flattened and crashed, so we used the gas dip to improve the next batch.

Why the gas dip works

The lower rate of moisture release during Phase 3 (the phase before first crack) is why the gas dip works: lowering the gas dramatically while evaporative cooling has slowed or paused helps to keep the ROR descending at a measured pace. Using

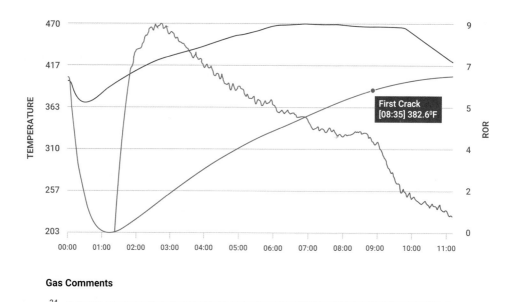

In roasting our first batch of this coffee, we progressively lowered the gas settings (orange graph), and the ROR flattened and crashed. The cup was baked, and we knew we could make the coffee juicier and sweeter.

a low gas setting also cools the roasting drum's metal temperature, allowing the roaster to safely increase the gas after the dip without concern for imparting harsh or roasty flavor on the coffee by overheating the drum surface. The higher-than-

How to time the gas dip during a roast

- Roast a batch of a coffee without using the gas dip.
- If the ROR crashes badly, the coffee may be a candidate for dipping.
- Set Cropster's ROR interval to 10s in RI3 (in Artisan, set the delta span to 5s or 10s) to view the curve with a fair amount of noise.
- Note the moment the crash began.
- Note the bean temperature 40–45 seconds before the crash (40 seconds for faster roasts, 45 for slower roasts).
- On the next batch, execute the dip at that bean temperature. (We'll call that the "dip temperature.")
- At the dip temperature, lower the gas by half for 20 seconds.
- After 20 seconds, return the gas to its pre-dip level.
- Do not drop the gas again until after first crack (usually around 9% DTR).

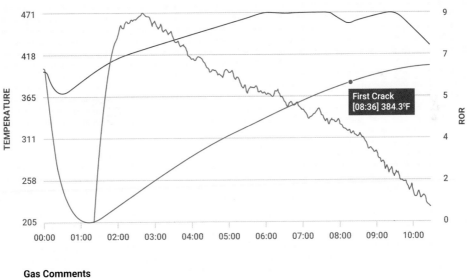

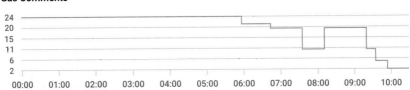

In the roast above, the orange gas graph shows that the roaster lowered the gas for 20 seconds and then, approximately 15 seconds before the anticipated crash, raised the gas back to the pre-dip level. As first crack faded, he lowered the gas incrementally to maintain a controlled, smoothly declining ROR.

usual gas setting after the dip helps carry the ROR curve through the "crash zone" with less risk of crashing.

Pro tips:
- If the ROR began to crash during the dip, the dip was too late.
- If the ROR rose to form a hump after the dip, the dip was too early.
- If the ROR smoothly declined during and after the dip, the dip was timed well.
- You may prefer to use slightly higher than usual gas settings pre-dip if doing that does not cause the ROR to flatten.
- After the gas dip, first crack will be more aggressive and the gas setting will be higher than it would usually be at that point in the roast. Therefore, when using the dip, taper the gas dramatically, usually beginning at 9% DTR.
- Some coffees crash at unusual times. For example, Ethiopians harvested in the past year have tended to crash more than a minute after the beginning of first crack. In such cases, it's appropriate to ignore first crack and simply apply gas settings as needed, where needed, to manage the ROR decline. You may even find yourself forced to dip well after first crack, and that's completely fine.

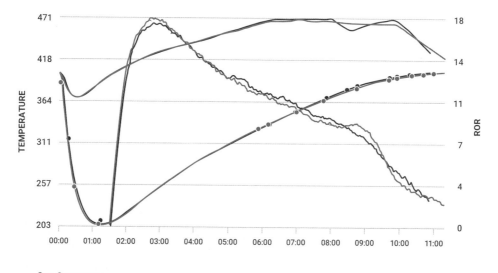

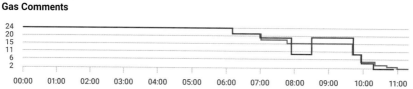

Here are the same two roasts with (red curves) and without (blue curves) the gas dip, shown on one graph. Note that the roaster used approximately the same total amount of gas for each roast but displaced the normal gas pattern during the gas dip, using less during the dip and a little more than usual in the areas around the dip.

Coffee Roasting: Best Practices

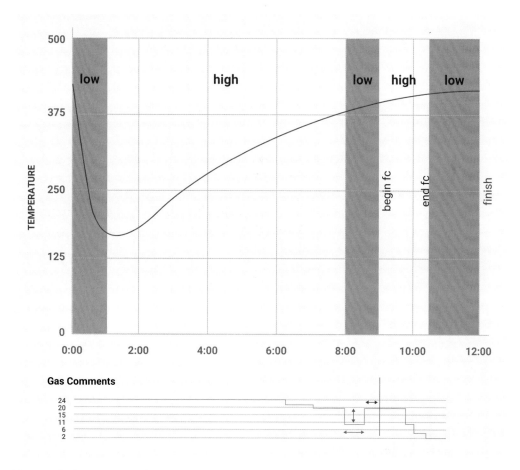

This graph shows Cropster's gas curve below the graph of the phases of moisture release. Note that the roaster dipped the gas just as the roast entered the phase of low moisture release. If one can time the dip to match that phase, the dip should create a smoothly declining ROR.

12

Marking First Crack Using the ETROR Curve

Note: Throughout the book I have used the term ROR (rate of rise) to refer to the bean temperature ROR (BTROR) during a roast. In this chapter, I introduce the term ETROR (environmental temperature ROR) and use the terms BTROR and ETROR to avoid confusion. In subsequent chapters, I revert to using "ROR" to denote BTROR.

Experienced roasters are aware that when first crack begins, the environmental temperature (ET) curve tends to rise. In 2018 it occurred to me that one could use the rise in the ET, or more precisely the dramatic increase in the ETROR (environmental temperature ROR) from a deep trough, to identify the beginning of first crack. This was a great discovery because up until then roasters had to rely almost exclusively on audible cues to mark the beginning of first crack. Given how difficult it is to hear the cracks in some machines, marking first crack based on sound can be unreliable.

I've never read an explanation of this phenomenon, so I'd like to speculate. As discussed in Chapter 11, beans release a great deal of moisture in a short period of time during first crack. The release of moisture, if not managed well, may lead to a *BTROR (bean temperature ROR)* crash. At first glance, it seems likely the (cooler) temperature of the released moisture is what causes the BTROR to drop, and it

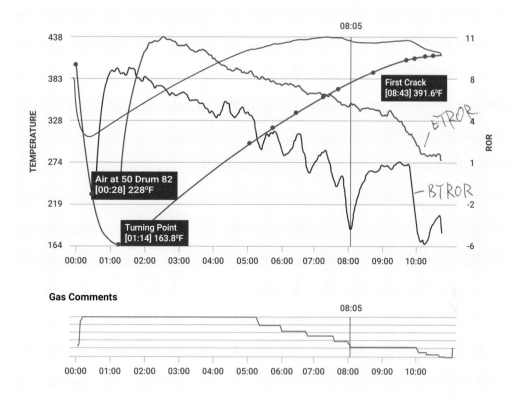

Some would look at this curve and argue that the decrease in gas shortly before the ETROR trough is what caused the trough. While lowering the gas surely contributed to the ETROR's decline, to even a casual observer this particular ETROR drop and rebound is obviously more dramatic than any other on the graph. That makes it a valid indicator of first crack. The roaster mistakenly marked first crack at 8:43, likely due to difficulty hearing the cracks.

probably is. But there is potentially another reason the BTROR drops: the rise in the ET/ETROR may indicate that the moisture released during first crack deflects hot air on its way from the burner to the bean pile. That would explain why the ETROR rises while the BTROR drops: the moisture acts like a force field, cooling the bean surfaces and deflecting incoming hot air.

I would argue that the moment the rise in the ETROR begins to accelerate is an objective indicator of the beginning of first crack. While not all coffees display a clear acceleration in ETROR (such as some decafs or naturals), the ETROR indicator works for the vast majority of coffees and roasting machines. In cases where the operator lowered the gas just before the ETROR curve bottomed out, one may have to use judgment to decide where to mark the beginning of first crack.

13

Odds and Ends

Strategies for indirectly heated roasters

When roasting on an indirectly heated machine, the general approach should be to steadily lower the gas while progressively increasing the fan speed. Such machines have a "burner box" maintained at temperatures much higher than roasting temperatures. I recommend first stabilizing at a consistent burner-box temperature before charging. During a batch, manage the burner-box temperature and the transfer of its heat to the roasting chamber by incrementally increasing the fan speed and lowering the gas. Once peak fan speed is reached, the burner-box temperature should decline in an effort to control the ROR descent. Unlike with most other types of roasting machines, indirectly heated machines require well-planned fan-speed adjustments to manage the balance of heat in the burner box and heat transferred to the roasting chamber. These machines can roast great coffee, but they require skillful airflow management.

Using electric roasters

I confess to not having as much experience as I would like in roasting on electric machines. The most successful approach in my limited experience is similar to the approach I recommend for indirectly heated roasters: progressively lower the heat while increasing the fan speed. One caveat about electric roasting is that compared with gas roasting, the burner temperature will have more *latency* as it is turned down. The roastmaster should compensate by lowering burner settings earlier or more aggressively. One can roast successfully on an electric machine, but it may require more careful planning and timing compared with roasting on a gas machine. If you plan to buy an electric roaster, I recommend seeking one with a low-latency burner.

Why I don't care to manage the time spent in the so-called Maillard phase

Roasters often ask me why I don't focus on manipulating time spent during the so-called Maillard phase during a roast. The answer is simple: whatever questionable benefit such manipulation may provide, one is better off focusing on achieving a smoothly declining ROR. An exceptionally long Maillard phase implies a lower, flatter ROR curve mid-roast, which will likely lead to a crash or, at least, a less-smooth ROR. Therefore, focusing on stretching the Maillard phase may increase the risk of baking coffee. Proponents of Maillard-phase manipulation should consider a few facts:

- The rate of Maillard reactions slows when one extends the time spent in the Maillard phase.

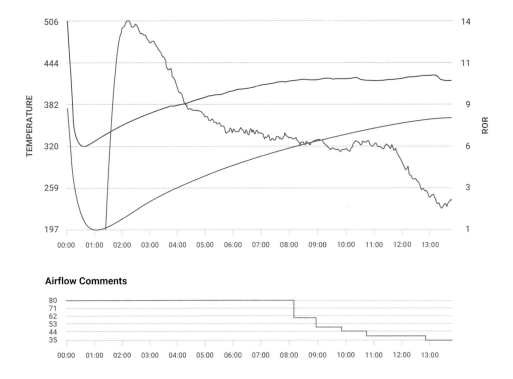

This roast had a long Maillard phase, and it is baked.

- It is impossible to know the beginning and end of the Maillard phase with accuracy.
- Intentional manipulation of the Maillard phase will usually come at the expense of a smoothly declining ROR. A smoothly declining ROR has more verifiable benefits in the cup.
- Time spent during the Maillard phase may not have a predictable effect on flavor because very fast and very slow roasts have different Maillard-phase lengths, yet they may taste quite similar.

Of course, if you roast two batches with different Maillard-phase lengths they will not taste the same. However, attributing those changes to the different times spent in the Maillard phase is too presumptive; those roasts will also have had different ROR curve shapes, and the shape of an ROR curve is a better predictor of flavor than is the duration of the Maillard phase.

Roasting for filter vs. espresso

I've been asked countless times whether one should approach roasting for filter and espresso differently. My usual answer is "perhaps, but I recommend focusing more on the difference in how you approach roasting for *black coffee* versus *white coffee*."

In my experience, most of the differences in the presumed ideal roasts for espresso and filter are due to differences in extraction. If you narrow the gap in the quality and quantity of your filter and espresso extractions, you will likely also narrow the gap in the roasts you perceive are ideal for each. For example, prior to popular adoption of the coffee refractometer, third-wave baristas routinely served sharp, sour, *underextracted ristretto* espressos extracted below 18% alongside balanced, 20% batch-brew extractions. In response, roasters offered darker espresso roasts to tone down the harsh acidity. Had baristas simply used longer espresso-brewing ratios, matching their espresso extraction levels those of their filter brews, they likely would have perceived less need for darker espresso roasts. Not coincidentally, as baristas later shifted to pulling higher-extraction espressos with more balance, roasters began lightening their espresso offerings.

At home on my DE1PRO espresso machine, I can pull espresso using techniques such as "blooming" and "pulsing" borrowed from filter brewing. With those tools in my espresso-making kit, I notice little difference in flavor balance compared with the filter coffee I brew using the same beans. At home I brew only very light roasts and use them interchangeably for espresso and filter brewing.

Roasting for "black coffee" vs. "white coffee"

An important distinction in roasting is the difference in approach when roasting for black coffee (espresso, Americano, filter) and white coffee (latte, cappuccino, other milky drinks). It's likely that the ideal flavor balance of a coffee to be consumed black is different from the ideal flavor balance of a coffee to be combined

with milk. Arguably, a less acidic roast with a greater amount of heavy compounds would complement milk better, while lighter, fruitier roasts would be better suited to being consumed black.

The bottom line is that one should roast differently for black coffee and white coffee. But how one approaches roasting for filter and espresso should be informed in part by differences in their extraction quality. An *omniroast* may be appropriate if one is able to extract filter and espresso to similar degrees and taste profiles. If extraction quality between the two varies too much, it may be wise to roast darker for espresso than for filter.

14

Post-Roast Quality Control

Color measurement

Measuring the color of roasted coffee can help estimate roast development. The outer-bean color indicates final roast color, and the color of the grounds is an estimate of inner-bean roast development.

When one can quantify the outer-bean color and the ground coffee color, one can calculate the "spread" between the two. The spread presumably indicates how uniformly the beans were roasted, though that is a matter of debate.

In my experience, the value of the data from the popular color-measurement devices is nearly identical, yet the cost of the machines varies dramatically. Before purchasing a color-measurement machine, please consider its cost, the value of its data, and how much ground coffee it requires you to consume per measurement. Some machines waste nearly 150 g of grounds per measurement; others waste 7 g per measurement. The cost difference over time can be staggering.

The Tonino probably wastes less ground coffee than any other device when taking a measurement.

Measuring weight loss

I recommend roasters measure the weight-loss percentage of every roast. Weight-loss calculations provide immediate feedback about roast development and consistency. For a given coffee with a consistent initial moisture content, greater weight loss indicates greater roast development.

(green weight - roasted weight) / green weight = weight loss %

Other indicators of roast development

This may seem prosaic, but simply biting or cracking open roasted beans with one's fingers can hint at roast development. Simply put, more developed beans are more brittle.

One can use extraction data—with caution—to estimate roast development. At light to medium roast levels, greater development of a given coffee will lead to higher average extraction levels. At darker roast levels, such as those dropped well after second crack has begun, beans lose some of their soluble material, and potential extraction levels decrease if one roasts dark enough.

Coffee Roasting: Best Practices

Using extraction data as a proxy for development is difficult. To be confident in the validity of the data, one first has to establish a baseline of repeatable extractions. In other words, if you brew a coffee ten times and always achieve extraction levels within a tight range (say, 21.0%–21.5%) and brews of a later roast batch of the same coffee consistently extract to only 20.0%–20.5%, you can be confident the development of the later batch was less. To be certain of your conclusion, I recommend that you return to the first batch and ensure its extraction is still within the original range, to eliminate the possibility that some brewing variable had drifted. If you have difficulty achieving such consistent extraction numbers, I recommend caution when extrapolating development information from extraction data.

15

Sample Roasting and Cupping

Sample roasting and cupping are the standard methods for evaluating green-coffee lots and making purchasing decisions. Cupping is also used to evaluate and compare production roasts. Sample roasting and cupping should ideally be "invisible" to the taster: one must roast and brew systematically, competently, and consistently, so as to not influence a taster's preference among several cups.

Sample roasting

The recent explosion in variety of sample roasters makes it difficult to offer specific advice about sample roasting. A traditional sample roast consists of a quick, light roast of 100 grams of coffee. Most sample roasters have ample power relative to the mass of a 100-g sample, so sample roasts are easy to develop, even in as little as 7 minutes.

While one cannot transfer roast profiles between sample roasters and produc-

tion roasters (see the next section), I strongly recommend using software such as Cropster or Artisan to log sample-roast data. Sample roasting is challenging because the roaster usually gets only one chance to roast an unfamiliar coffee. If the data shows a sample roast did not go well (for example, the ROR crashed hard), the cupper may consider either asking for a replacement sample or being more generous when scoring the poorly roasted sample.

What you can (and can't) learn from a sample roast's data

Despite persistent rumors to the contrary, it is impossible to transfer a roast profile from a sample roaster to a production roaster. As mentioned, bean-temperature data is not an objective, accurate representation of the beans' surface tempera- tures. The bean probe's own mass and location, as well as the air temperature sur- rounding the probe, affect its reading. Even if a sample roast and production roast of a coffee share the same duration and have similar data collected by identical probes, the resulting cups would taste different.

What you *can* learn from a sample roast is more general information about a coffee's behavior in the roaster. If you take a standard approach to all sample roasts (always using the same batch size, charge temperature, and nearly identi- cal gas settings, etc.), the results will hint at the coffee's behavior relative to other beans, such as how much energy it requires to roast, if and when its ROR is likely to crash, and when first crack occurs. That information offers insight into how much gas to use in a production roast and hints at when events may occur.

How to cup

Cupping is the worldwide standard quality-control protocol for tasting and evaluating samples of green coffee or production roasts. You may be tempted to assess quality by other brewing methods, but I recommend initially tasting each sample by cupping.

Cupping is convenient when one needs to compare large numbers of samples, and it is arguably the easiest brewing method to do well—it requires no specialized equipment or filters and it runs no risk of *channeling* the way *percolation* brewing does. *Channels* cause *astringency*, which interferes with one's ability to make a fair comparison between cups.

When evaluating green samples for purchase, it's critical to roast all of the samples as similarly as possi-

Coffee Roasting: Best Practices

ble and to brew them identically so that differences among the cups are due only to the green quality. A simple, easily repeatable cupping protocol is essential.

Standard cupping procedure:
- Boil ample water.
- Grind 7–12 g of coffee on a medium-fine setting (11:00–11:30 on an EK dial or, for the uber-geeks: a particle-size peak of approximately 500 microns).
- Tare the cupping cups (or bowls).
- Pour the water when it is a few degrees below boiling (approximately 207°F/97°C).
- Use 17 times more water than grounds, by weight. For example, if you use 10 g of grounds, use 170 g of water per bowl.
- Set a timer as you begin pouring the first bowl. Pour the remaining bowls.
- Fill a few "rinse cups" with hot water to rinse spoons during cupping.
- At 4:00, "break the crust" of the first bowl by skimming the surface of the bowl with the back of a spoon.
- Sniff the aroma released and churn the crust to submerge it.
- Break the crusts and submerge the grounds of the remaining bowls, in the order in which they were poured.
- Survey the bowls and remove any remaining surface sludge.
- Begin slurping at some point between 11:00–13:00 when the coffee temperature is comfortable.
- Forcefully slurp partial spoonfuls, spraying the coffee throughout your oral cavity. Slurp samples from each bowl several times, taking notes as you go.
- Return to the bowls in 30–60 minutes, when they have cooled to room temperature, and repeat the process.

Notes:
- Weigh the grounds to a resolution of 0.1 g.
- The water weight may vary by a few grams per bowl. That won't affect the results meaningfully if the ground weight is precise to within 0.1 g.
- Cupping spoons should have round, deep bowls.
- Spraying the coffee throughout your oral cavity creates more coffee-droplet surface area, which increases the aromatic impression of the coffee.
- It's important to cup when the coffee is warm and again when it has cooled. Some defects are easier to detect at cooler temperatures.
- After each slurp from a spoon, dip the spoon into the rinse cup and tap the spoon dry on a dish towel on the cupping table.
- Carry a spittoon or have one handy to prevent over-caffeination. Spit after each slurp.

Cupping procedure is loosely standardized, whether done at a roastery in the US or at a green-coffee auction in Kenya. The procedure below is what I consider the norm. You're likely to encounter similar, often less precise, cupping protocols if you work in coffee and you cup in a variety of locations.

Cupping "espresso roasts"

Many roasters don't bother to cup roasts meant for espresso. I think this is a mistake, as cupping is the most effective way to evaluate roast quality, regardless of the intended brewing method. Espresso extraction is a fickle process, and it is easy to mistakenly reject a good roast due to a subpar extraction. Cupping may not indicate precisely how a coffee will taste as a shot of espresso, but it is the most reliable way to evaluate

roast quality. If a roast cups well but doesn't perform well as espresso, it's worth investigating whether the extraction is at fault.

To offer a roast the best chance of success as a shot of espresso, you should *degas* the beans enough to prevent underextraction. For fresh beans roasted within the past few days, grind the beans 40–60 minutes before pulling them as espresso. Alternatively, age roasts in whole-bean form for 10–15 days and pull shots immediately after grinding.

Cupping right out of the roaster

When I'm on a consulting job, I'm under pressure to immediately improve a client's roasts. It's not always practical for me to wait a day to cup roasts, adjust and roast them again, and wait yet another day to taste the new batches. Done properly, cupping coffee immediately after roasting can provide a quicker feedback loop when adjusting roast curves.

When cupping right out of the roaster, it's critical to ensure the bean cores are cool before grinding. While the bean surfaces may feel cool to the touch after 3 or 4 minutes in the cooling bin, the bean cores may require an additional minute

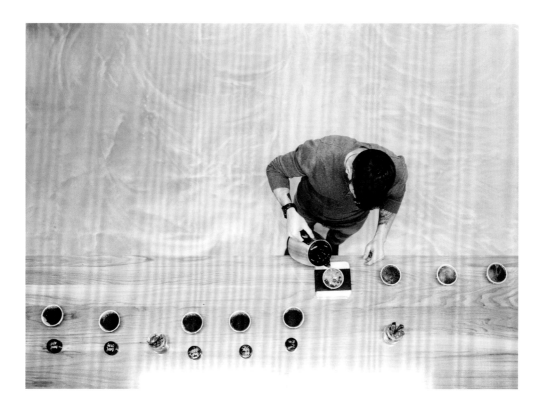

or two in the cooling bin to reach room temperature. Warm beans are less brittle and won't shatter properly in the grinder; they will produce hollow, savory, and unpleasant flavors. Even when the beans are fully cooled and safe to grind, they won't taste identical to how they will a day later, but the cupping results will be valid enough to hint at how to adjust the next batch of the coffee. Baked, under-developed, and roasty flavors are easy to detect when cupping within minutes of roasting. When one needs to roast numerous consecutive batches of the same coffee, the immediate feedback provided by cupping right out of the roaster can help the roaster incrementally improve each batch.

16

Bean Storage

Green-coffee packaging

When I began roasting coffee, all green coffee was delivered in loosely woven burlap sacks that did little to protect the coffee from aromatic taints or changes in moisture. Over the past 15 years, it has become standard to ship quality coffee in hermetically sealed plastic bags, such as GrainPro. While packing coffee in plastic costs an extra few cents per kilogram, it is a bargain, as it limits loss of quality during shipping and slows the aging process of coffee. Plastic bags can easily prevent the loss of one or two "points" from a coffee's green score during shipping. Each point in the specialty-coffee range is worth $0.15–$0.75 USD per pound (depending on market conditions), so plastic packaging is an excellent investment. Even if you buy sub-specialty-grade coffee, plastic packaging still offers an excellent return on your investment.

Green storage and longevity

The colder the storage conditions, the slower green coffee ages. At the extreme, frozen green hardly ages at all, and it stays fresh for many years. While I'm not recommending that all roasters freeze their green, I recommend storing green coffee at colder temperatures (such as in a basement) if you plan to hold it for more than 4–6 weeks. Room temperature is reasonable for short-term storage. Most importantly, try to avoid exposing green coffee to temperatures above 80°F (27°C) for extended periods of time, as the green will age noticeably faster than it will at room temperature.

Green storage and roast repeatability

Whatever temperature you choose for long-term green storage, I recommend holding coffee at or near room temperature for at least three days before roasting. It's critical to stabilize the temperature of the green for long enough to ensure the inner and outer bean temperature is homogenous prior to roasting.

Roasted-coffee storage

Roasted beans age more rapidly than green coffee. The same principles that apply to storing green coffee apply to roasted coffee: sealed bags and colder temperatures protect the coffee and retard aging. Store beans at room temperature in a tightly sealed container if you plan to use them within a week or two of roasting.

Freezing extends shelf life by years if done properly. Compared with room-temperature beans, frozen coffee is more brittle and produces more fines when ground. That's acceptable for espresso, so it's reasonable to use frozen beans for

espresso making. Extra fines are undesirable in filter brewing, so I recommend thawing frozen beans before grinding for filter.

If you choose to freeze coffee beans at home for filter brewing, I recommend sealing them in small portions and thawing each sealed portion to room temperature before exposing it to air and grinding. If you're a prolific bean freezer, consider investing in a small vacuum-sealing machine for optimal long-term bean storage.

Storing ground coffee

While almost all of us in the specialty coffee field grind beans immediately before brewing, it's common for wholesale customers of coffee roasters, such as restaurants, to request pre-ground coffee. To accommodate those customers, I recommend packing ground coffee in vacuum-sealed portion packs. If you want to "go the extra mile," you can nitrogen-flush the air in the packs or insert an oxygen-absorbing pad into each pack. Coffee packaged in this way will taste fresh for months, but it must be brewed immediately after the customer opens the pack, as the coffee will degrade rapidly.

17

Common Roasting Mistakes and Hindrances

These are some of the most common roasting mistakes I encounter. Each of them is easily remedied.

Too much data smoothing

While some smoothing is necessary to make sense out of noisy temperature data, many roasters smooth data to such an extreme that they lose much of its value. Some roasters favor smoother data because it hides mistakes and small inconsistencies. But if you care more about how your coffee tastes than how your data looks, you should always attempt to use as little smoothing as is necessary, but no more.

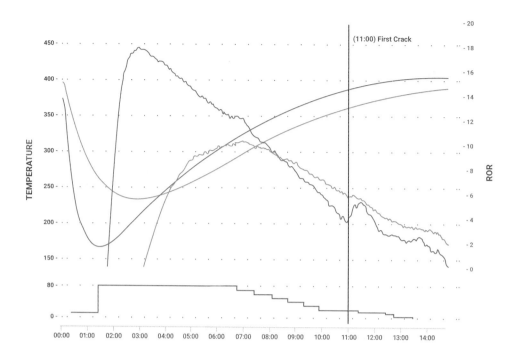

Thick probes

The effect of using an unnecessarily thick probe is similar to that of applying too much data smoothing. I recommend using probes with diameters between 2.5–4 mm to collect data with a reasonable balance of speed and noise. As discussed, thicker probes have more mass, which slows their response time and yields smooth, delayed data. In the graph above, the same batch was tracked by a 3-mm probe (blue curves) and a 10-mm probe (yellow curves). Note how the ROR from the 3-mm probe showed a problematic hump after first crack, but the 10-mm probe smoothed the data so much that the hump didn't appear.

Roasting too many different batch sizes

Sometimes the logistics of running an efficient business conflict with efforts to roast the best possible coffee. One of the most common such conflicts involves choosing what batch sizes to roast. Ideally, a roaster would roast only one batch size and never vary it. Roasting just one batch size makes it easier to master a coffee and the ideal BBP for that batch size. Switching between batch sizes of a coffee during a roasting session requires mastering more than one curve for a given coffee and also requires a specialized BBP to shift the roasting machine's thermal energy to the appropriate level for the new batch size. Getting such a transitional BBP just right is extremely difficult.

I realize there are times when a roaster needs to roast more than one batch size. My advice is to do your best to limit batch-size variety, attempt to standardize your roasts to two batch sizes at most, and put effort into mastering the transitional BBP.

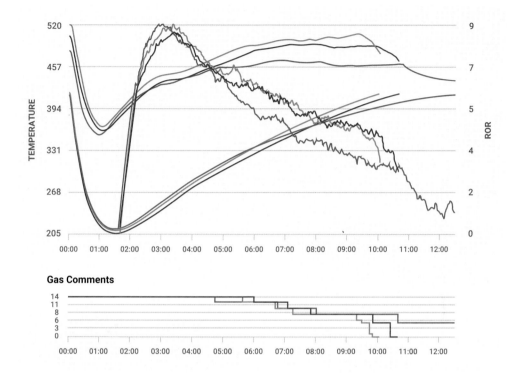

Gas Comments

The graph above shows three consecutive batches of the same coffee, using the same initial gas settings, etc. Although the turn is not "real" data, if a roaster uses an effective BBP to roast consecutive batches, the bean curves should map each other perfectly through the turn.

Inconsistent or ineffective between-batch protocol

It's a poorly kept secret in the coffee industry that few roasters are reliably consistent. The first step in consistent roasting is to use an effective between-batch protocol (BBP). When one uses a good BBP with precision, roast curves will "trace" each other, with no gap between them. (See Chapter 5 for examples.)

Self-satisfaction, inadequate blind cupping, and cupping of others' coffees

Roasters, even new ones, tend to be very confident. Not a few novice roasters, despite having a mere few weeks of experience, have told me that they were among the top 10% of roasters in their country. Many roasters become fans, rather than critics, of their own product, and that slows their progress. As a coffee lover, it's natural to want to buy a cup, relax, and enjoy it for what it is. But when consuming your own coffee as a professional, it's essential to always ask, "How could this coffee have been better?" Self-inquiry and honest criticism are keys to progress.

A roaster can use some tools to critically analyze his own coffee and maintain a balanced perspective. These include cupping with a diverse group of partners, always cupping blindly, frequently cupping other roasters' coffees (blindly) on the same table as your own, and seeking feedback from more-experienced coffee professionals whenever possible.

18

Roasting Software and Automation

Types of roasting software

You can choose from among several types of roasting software:
- Simple, free data-logging software *(freeware)*
- Sophisticated freeware for data logging and other tasks
- Commercial *roastery management solutions*
- *Integrated software*

Simple data-logging freeware (for non-techies)

As discussed earlier in this book, data-logging software has played a pivotal role in helping roasters master their craft. If you're a home roaster merely seeking to roast great coffee, free data-logging software may meet your needs.

Sophisticated freeware for data logging and other tasks

For those with some technical skills who want to not just log roast data but also to create reference curves, analyze their roast data from various angles, and have highly customizable settings, more sophisticated freeware, such as Artisan, is the best choice.

Commercial roastery management solutions

Roastery management solutions (RMS) are commercial software packages that offer traditional data logging integrated with many efficiency-enhancing features such as tech support, automatic inventory control, and production planning. Cropster is the best-known example of this type of software.

Integrated software

Machine manufacturers (Probat, Diedrich, Giesen, etc.) offer various types of built-in or add-on roast-control software. Such integrated software usually offers crude data logging and roast automation. Many of my clients who have purchased integrated software with their new machines have been frustrated by the software's limited utility and have chosen to use Cropster or Artisan instead, despite having paid for the integrated software. I believe roasting-machine manufacturers felt competitive pressure to offer proprietary software, but their offerings usually lagged behind those of dedicated software companies. Manufacturers and RMS suppliers have begun forming partnerships in the past two years, which is a hopeful sign that the roasting-software market is maturing and integrated software may improve more quickly.

Some integrated software is worth using. I prefer not to name brands, but if readers are interested in integrated software, I recommend working with companies that offer ecosystems of compatible products (hardware, software, data management) rather than ones offering integrated software as a late, expensive add-on. If you're considering adding integrated software to your new roasting machine, be sure to "take the software for a test drive" and to log the test batches simultaneously with Cropster to provide a helpful, critical view of the results.

How to choose software for your needs

To choose the best solution, consider these questions:
- Is roasting your business? Is it costly to have to stop production when there are problems? Commercial RMS is likely the best option.
- Are you a do-it-yourself home roaster simply wanting to track roast data to improve quality on a small machine? Simple freeware is probably all you need.
- Do you want to roast, create reference curves, and analyze several roasts at one time? All options may work, but most integrated software offers poor data resolution, and freeware often requires technical skills to master all of its features. Here, RMS is probably the best solution for the average user, and freeware may be an option for the more technically inclined user.
- In addition to data logging and roast analysis, do you want to track green-coffee inventory, green samples, blend components, and various quality-control variables? RMS is the best option.

Roast control and automation

Roasting machines and software packages range from fully manual to fully automatic, with various semiautomated options in between. I love the idea of automating as much of the process as possible. Before you wrinkle your nose in judgment, consider that we already outsource almost all of the roasting process to sensors, valves, burners, fans, computers, and so on. I'm not being cheeky— most opponents of automation conveniently ignore that we already rely on machines to monitor the process and to do almost all of the work. Automation is the future of roasting, but efforts to implement more of it have thus far often been disappointing.

Manual roasting

Manual roasting involves the operator pulling levers, turning dials, or pushing buttons to change gas and airflow settings during a roast. While one can manually roast amazing coffee, human error and small inconsistencies make manual roasts difficult to repeat with precision. If you prefer to roast manually, ensure that your controls and instrumentation offer reasonable precision.

Recipe software systems (semiautomated control)

These systems allow the user to program a gas and airflow "recipe" prior to loading a batch, and the software executes the settings based on time or bean-temperature triggers during a roast. In the right hands, such systems outperform any current automated system I have seen. The only caveat about recipe systems is that one may often be better off manually controlling a roast after first crack, depending on the system's features and precision.

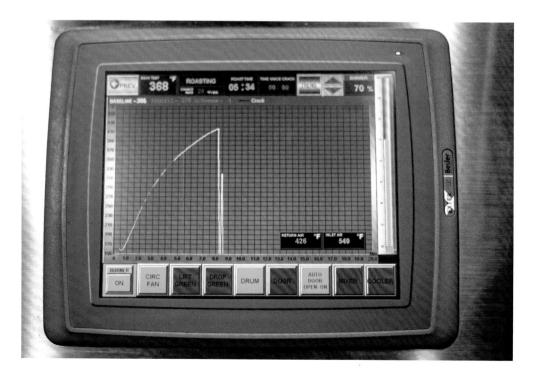

Coffee Roasting: Best Practices

Recipe systems are now offered as part of some integrated software systems (such as Probat Pilot), sophisticated freeware (such as Artisan, which is useful if you have some serious tech skills), and RMS systems such as Cropster's Gas Control & Replay Assist. If you choose a recipe system, ensure that it allows you to pre-program a reasonably large number of settings per roast. (Some older, integrated systems limit the user to just 3–5 gas settings per roast, which is not enough.)

Automated profiling systems (fully automatic control)

Most automated profiling systems seek to replicate a past roast curve by making microadjustments in gas and air settings throughout a batch. In theory, such systems should be superior to any other. In practice, most profiling systems I've seen have fallen short of their promise. They often overshoot and undershoot temperature targets by unacceptable margins, overreact if the target temperature and current temperature are too far apart, and adjust gas settings up and down in small, rapid bursts, a method that can rob coffee of sweetness.

One can add a third-party automation system to a roasting machine, but in my experience, those systems are buggy and require many hours of adjustment by a dedicated tech. If you are determined to buy a fully automated system, my advice is the same as it was about buying integrated software: seek a company offering an ecosystem of compatible products (hardware, software, data management); take the equipment for a "test drive" before purchasing it; and log the data in parallel using Cropster for a thorough post-roast analysis. (I recommend tracking the trial data with Cropster because Cropster's high-resolution view of the data may help you spot mistakes made by the automated software.)

19

Software Setup and Troubleshooting

Things to consider before connecting your roaster

If you are using only your machine's built-in, integrated software, and nothing else, to control the roaster and log data, your system should work properly right out of the box. You won't need this chapter.

If you have chosen any sort of add-on software to use with your machine, I offer you this chapter. Written with the help of the fine, experienced folks at Cropster, it will help you connect software to your roaster and troubleshoot problems.

What you'll need to connect

When connecting third-party software, you'll need a PC or Mac (post-2013) with +4GB of RAM, a +500GB hard drive, an internet connection, an available USB port, and a +15-inch screen that supports high resolution (+1080 pixels). You'll also need a robust internet signal at your roastery.

Choosing a computer for your roastery

Roasteries are dusty. Laptops and smaller computers run cooler than larger machines and collect less dust, so they tend to be better options for roasteries.

Screen size matters. The larger the screen, the more detail you'll see in the data, especially when you are farther from the screen. I recommend getting a very large screen. Not only will it give you a better view of your roasting data, but if you roast in a café, the screen would make a great prop to engage customers and interest them in the roasting process.

How to connect your computer

If you opt for a manufacturer's integrated profiler, you will have limited profiling available immediately. If you are connecting a computer and a third-party software solution, there are a few possible ways to connect the software and roasting machine.

- If your roaster has Ethernet or Wi-Fi, you can use either to connect to your laptop. Given the choice, an Ethernet cable is more reliable than a Wi-Fi signal. If using Wi-Fi, follow the software developer's instructions to find your roasting machine on your Wi-Fi network.
- If your roasting machine has a USB connection, you need a USB cable. It's usually a good idea to keep this cable under 10 ft. (3 m) long to ensure a steady connection.
- If your roasting machine lacks Wi-Fi, Ethernet, and a USB port, you will need a data bridge such as a "Phidget" to connect your temperature probes to the software.

How to confirm everything is working

Once you have connected the software and the roasting machine, confirm that the information your computer sees is in sync with the information the roasting machine presents.

- Check whether all expected values (bean temperature, environmental temperature, etc.) are shown on the screen. If not, activate them in the "settings" section of the software.
- Compare the temperature values you see on your computer with the values shown on the roasting machine. They should match.
- Do a test roast and check whether the curve is in sync with your machine's settings.
- After completing the roast, check that the software synced and saved the data properly.

Troubleshooting connections and data

If the software does not connect to the machine or the data seems unusual or inconsistent, consider these troubleshooting steps:

- Check all of your physical connections.
- Consider whether anything was recently changed, moved, updated, replaced, etc.
- Turn the power source for everything off for 15–20 seconds and then on again—support people may joke about this, but it often works. When powering everything back on, turn on the computer before you turn on the roasting machine.
- Contact your supplier or support people. If you're using freeware, seek help on an online forum.

Expert hints and simple mistakes to avoid

An expert is a man who has made all the mistakes which can be made, in a narrow field.
   —Niels Bohr

The folks at Cropster have seen it all and offer these simple, hard-won bits of advice:
- Know your sensors. Are you using a J- or K-type thermocouple or a different standard, such as RTD?
- Grounded probes have a tendency to collect interference, especially if you spliced wires. A good way to tell if your probe is grounded is to take it out of its fitting and touch it to the machine face (while the machine is powered on). Each touch should result in a temperature spike to above room temperature. It is best to avoid using grounded probes.
- Swapping + and − on a thermocouple will result in temperature readings changing in the wrong direction. This happens often during installations.
- Thermocouples age and lose accuracy over time. Keep that in mind, and plan to replace them every few years.
- Static: If you are going to splice wires, wear rubber sneakers and touch something metal before you begin. Static can damage electrical devices.
- When playing with wires, first disconnect the USB/Ethernet from your computer and power off your roasting machine.
- When connecting your machine via Wi-Fi or Ethernet, confirm that the connection works while the setup technician is present.

Glossary

Airflow The passage of air from one area to another. Airflow is the primary means of heat transfer and pollution removal during coffee roasting.

Artisan Popular free software used for coffee roasting and other data-logging activities.

Astringency The tactile sensation of dryness in one's mouth after consuming a certain food or drink.

Baked (flavors) Hollow, straw-like flavors in coffee resulting from a roast curve's "rate of rise" dropping rapidly.

Bean-temperature curve (bean curve) The graphical display of bean-temperature data points throughout the duration of a roast batch.

Bean-temperature probe (bean probe) A device that measures surface coffee-bean temperature during roasting.

Between-batch protocol A method of managing and resetting a roasting machine's thermal energy between batches.

Black coffee A coffee beverage made without any type of milk.

Bulk density measurement A simple, imprecise method to measure the density of a substance, such as coffee beans.

Caramelization The browning of sugar.

Carbonization The conversion of an organic substance into carbon. Also, the process by which coffee beans acquire a black color during roasting.

Channeling The formation of larger, higher-flow paths through the coffee bed during percolation brewing.

Charge The moment of dropping coffee beans into a roasting machine to begin a batch.

Classic-drum roaster A design of coffee-roasting machine featuring a horizontal, rotating drum suspended above a gas burner or other heat source.

Conductive heat transfer The transfer of heat by direct contact.

Convective heat transfer The transfer of heat by the movement of fluids.

Cropster A popular brand of software for coffee roasting and roastery management.

Cupper/cupping Cupping, practiced by cuppers, is the standard coffee-industry method of tasting and evaluating coffee.

Damper A mechanical device used to restrict airflow in a coffee-roasting machine.

Degas To release gas, as roasted coffee beans do during storage.

Delta span (ROR interval) The period of time over which data points are averaged to create an ROR curve.

Derivative In calculus, the rate of change of any variable with respect to any other. In coffee roasting, the rate of rise (ROR) curve is the derivative of the bean-temperature curve.

Development time The time from the onset of first crack until the end of a roast batch.

Development time ratio (DTR) A roast's development time relative to its total duration.

Displacement measurement (for density) A method of calculating an object's density.

Electric roaster A roasting machine with an electric burner element as its heat source.

Environmental temperature (ET) The temperature of the air as it leaves the drum during coffee roasting.

Environmental temperature rate of rise (ETROR) In coffee roasting, the rate of change of the environmental temperature per unit of time. Roasters often use the ETROR curve to discern the beginning of first crack.

Evaporative cooling Cooling caused by the evaporation of water, such as on the surfaces of coffee beans during roasting.

Flick Coffee-industry slang for an increase in the ROR curve at the end of a roast.

First crack A phase of coffee roasting characterized by loud popping noises due to the release of pressure and water vapor from within the beans.

Freeware Software that is available at no cost to the consumer.

Gas dip A method of manipulating gas application to prevent ROR crashes during coffee roasting.

Green coffee Coffee in its raw state, not yet roasted.

Inches of water column The amount of pressure required to raise a column of water one inch.

Indirectly heated drum roaster A roasting-machine design in which the burner flame is not in direct contact with the drum.

Inlet temperature (IT) In coffee roasting, the temperature of the air as it enters the roasting drum from the burner.

Integrated software Built-in or add-on roast-control software offered by roasting-machine manufacturers.

Latency The time delay between cause and effect. In the case of a coffee-bean temperature probe, its lag in response time to changes in bean temperature.

Maillard reactions Chemical reactions between amino acids and reducing sugars that contribute to coffee's brown color and roasty flavors.

Manometer An instrument for measuring the pressure of liquids and gases.

Mixing vane Paddle-like protrusions that agitate and mix coffee beans in a roasting drum.

Moisture content In coffee roasting, the percent of a bean's weight made up of water.

Omniroast Coffee-industry slang for when a roaster or barista uses the same roast or roast degree for both espresso and filter coffee.

Percolation In the case of coffee brewing, the passage of water through a bed of coffee grounds to extract soluble material into the liquid.

Production roast A batch of coffee roasted for sale, as opposed to one roasted merely for evaluation.

ROR crash A near-vertical drop in an ROR curve during roasting.

ROR curve (ROR or BTROR) A curve representing the change in the bean temperature per unit of time during coffee roasting.

ROR interval (delta span) The period of time over which data points are averaged to create an ROR curve.

RTD A thermometer type used in coffee roasting. RTDs measure temperature change by sensing the change in electrical resistance of metals.

Ristretto A shot of espresso pulled "short" or using a low ratio of water to grounds.

Roast development The process of breaking down beans' cellulose during coffee roasting.

Roastery management solutions (RMS) Commercial software packages that offer traditional data logging integrated with efficiency-enhancing features such as tech support, automatic inventory control, and production planning.

Sample roast A small roast batch, usually of 100 g, typically done to evaluate whether to buy an offering of green coffee.

Sample roaster A roasting machine that accommodates batches ranging from 50 g to 500 g in size.

Scorching The burning of the surfaces of the beans during a roast.

Second crack A phase during a dark roast in which the release of carbon dioxide from the beans creates loud popping noises.

Soak A method in which the roaster users a low gas setting for the first minute or two of a roast batch before increasing the gas setting.

Stall In coffee roasting, the moment at which the bean temperature stops increasing.

Thermal conductivity A measure of how well a material conducts heat.

Thermal energy The energy, contained in a system, that determines its temperature.

Thermal lag In coffee roasting, the delay in a change in a temperature probe's reading.

Thermocouple Temperature sensors that convert the voltage produced between two metals to a local temperature reading.

Third-wave roast Generally understood in the coffee industry to be a light roast of a specialty-grade coffee.

Tipping Burn marks at the long ends of "tips" of coffee beans.

Trier (trowel) A scoop, mounted on the faceplate of a coffee roaster, for sampling beans during roasting.

Turning point ("the turn") The low point in a typical bean-temperature curve during coffee roasting.

Underdeveloped A term for roasted coffee with bean centers neither sufficiently cooked nor broken down.

Underextracted Insufficient removal of soluble material during coffee brewing.

Ungrounded In relation to thermocouples, one in which the junction and sheath do not touch; this design prevents a "ground loop," an undesirable source of data noise.

Water activity (a_w) As per Wikipedia, the partial vapor pressure of water in a substance divided by the standard state partial vapor pressure of water. In my layman's terms, the amount of unbound water in a food relative to its bound water.

White coffee Australian slang for a coffee beverage, such as a cappuccino, made with milk.